Jeff Gordon

Jeff Gordon
An Unauthorized Biography

Gary L. Thomas

RENAISSANCE BOOKS

LOS ANGELES

Library of Congress Cataloging-in-Publication Data
Thomas, Gary.
    Jeff Gordon : an unauthorized biography / Gary Thomas.
        p.   cm.
    Includes bibliographical references (p.) and index.
    ISBN 1-58063-091-X
    1. Gordon, Jeff, 1971– . 2. Automobile racing drivers—United
States Biography. I. Title.
GV1032.G67T47 1999
796.72'092—dc21
    [B]   99-37893
                                              CIP

10 9 8 7 6 5 4 3 2 1

Design by James Tran and Lisa-Theresa Lenthall
Typesetting by James Tran

Published by Renaissance Books
Distributed by St. Martin's Press
Manufactured in the United States of America
First Edition

Acknowledgments

I'd like to thank Carol Bickford (Jeff Gordon's mom) and John Bickford Sr. (Jeff's stepdad) for graciously giving me their time and comments. I'd also like to thank my agent, Scott Waxman, and editor, Jim Parish, for making this book possible.

Contents

chapter 1

Jockeying for Position

"Right now, Jeff [Gordon] is as good as there is 'cause he's out there doin' it. With what he's done, the way he's come into this sport, he's a winner."

—Legendary stock-car driver Richard Petty, 1998

Jeff Gordon wasn't even born yet, but already he was in the race of his life. It took him over twenty-four hours just to travel down his mother's birth canal that August day in 1971. Twenty-five years later, however, Gordon would be famous for his high speed; he would consistently demonstrate his ability to race five hundred miles on high-banked curves in roughly three hours.

Carol Gordon (now Carol Bickford), Jeff's mom, had hints about the future racer's personality while he was still in utero. Her first child, Kim, had entered the world a few years earlier after a smooth and quiet pregnancy. Kim was a calm and easygoing baby; she rarely cried and Carol actually had to wake Kim to feed her.

Jeff was anything but quiet. "Jeff was very active in and out [of the womb]," Carol laughs. But when it was time for Jeff to make his appearance, the kid just wouldn't budge.

Carol's labor with Jeff was extremely difficult, and the hospital in Vallejo, California (near San Francisco), didn't seem all that well prepared. Nurses had to fashion a makeshift girdle out of a bedsheet, hoping to force the baby down, but Jeff was about as stubborn as an infant could be.

Finally the doctor gave up and suggested a C-section in the morning.

"Fine," Carol said.

But Jeff had other ideas.

The doctor gave Carol an injection to relax her so that she could gather strength for the morning operation. He then left the hospital and Carol fell asleep. The next thing Carol knew, a nurse was shaking her awake: "Carol! Carol! Wake up!"

Jeff was ready to be born, and the doctor was now too far away to make it back to the hospital. Years later, Jeff would be known for making an improbable charge from way back in the pack and somehow taking the lead near the end, and that's exactly how he was born on August 4, 1971. Just when everybody was counting him out, he came racing on to the scene, creating near-bedlam in the hospital.

The nurse couldn't get Carol on the gurney to wheel her into the delivery room by herself, so she rushed outside to find help. A few nurses joined her, and they finally got Jeff's mom rolling.

But Jeff was in a hurry, and as soon as it became apparent that the once reluctant baby was now racing toward the world at a speed faster than the doctor could match in his car, they located a midwife. She had barely arrived before she was holding Jeff's naked body in her hands.

Carol and Jeff's father, Will Gordon, were divorced when Jeff was just three months old, and Carol soon realized she had her hands full raising such an active child on her own. "Jeff was a challenging child," Carol told me some months ago over a cup of coffee. "He didn't know the meaning of the word 'no.'" It wasn't a matter of Carol's discipline skills. Jeff's older sister Kim had fallen in line from the day she was delivered, but Jeff was always out to push the boundaries.

When Jeff was just a toddler, Carol took him to a friend's house. The woman had a glass coffee table, and Jeff liked to pull himself up on it, which would leave behind a mess of fingerprints. Carol's friend said, "No, Jeffrey, no," and Jeff started shaking all over—but he wouldn't stop. Not until she made him.

"'No' just did not register with him," Carol's friend remembers.

But "difficult" doesn't mean "bad." Though strong willed, Jeff had a "cleaner" childhood than most adolescents—in part because of his focus on racing, which left him little time to get into serious trouble.

"He just required a lot of attention," Carol explains. "He didn't want to be read to. He always wanted to be *doing* something. He always had to be occupied. He got bored quickly, so he was constantly moving from one thing to another."

It's not hard to imagine a NASCAR driver-in-training.

The Birth of a Dynasty

Today Jeff Gordon has an all-star, all-American look about him. His dark hair is thick and commanding, his eyebrows hefty and coarse. He sports a cleft chin and an almost statuesque square jaw. In 1997, he was chosen one of *People* magazine's "50 Most Beautiful People in the World." His wife, Brooke, told the publication, "Women come up to me all the time and say, 'You're so lucky you got him before I could.' I just laugh. I agree with them. He's the best-looking thing I've laid eyes on."

What he lacks in height (standing at just five feet seven inches), Jeff works to overcome with strength, adopting strenuous fitness goals. However, he insists he doesn't care two lug nuts about image. "All I try to do is make my hair look good," he informed *People,* "and let the rest just fall in place."

Some sports enthusiasts seem close to hatred in their regard for the number 24 driver. His fans are legion, but his detractors are fierce, and have even endangered his life on one or two occasions. One racing fan told *Newsweek,* "No sir, I didn't come here to watch a wreck. I don't want to see nobody get hurt, that's for sure, even if it's Jeff Gordon."

But true racing experts realize that there is something rare about Gordon. Richard Petty (often referred to as "the King" by racing fans for his record number of wins) readily admitted late in 1998, "Right now, Jeff is as good as there is 'cause he's out there doin' it. With what he's done, the way he's come into this sport, he's a winner."

Three championships in four years, over forty wins, and he's not even thirty years old. . . . You can't argue with success. No other driver in the current top-ten of the National Association for Stock-Car Auto Racing (NASCAR) field won a race before he was twenty-seven. "Think about that," journalist Steve Ballard writes. "[Dale] Earnhardt, Mark Martin, Rusty Wallace, Dale Jarrett, Terry Labonte—at the age Gordon is now, the sum total of their [NASCAR Winston Cup] victories was zero."

With such drive and success, you might think the young, "difficult" boy might grow up to be an egomaniac, but those close to him testify to an unusually sensitive man with a sure grounding. Gordon's stepfather, John Bickford Sr. raves about Jeff's "tremendous self-confidence, relentless desire to succeed, and a surprising degree of humility."

Whatever your opinion of Jeff, he clearly represents the future of NASCAR. "Gordon came at the perfect time," triumphs the legendary Charlotte (North Carolina) Motor Speedway president Humpy Wheeler. (In February 1999, Charlotte Motor Speedway's name was officially changed to Lowe's Motor Speedway. Since most of the events in this book predate this change, the former name will be used throughout.)

Jeff's style, his size, and his team all have peaked and blossomed at exactly the right time. In the days before power steering it took a big man to steer a stock car for five hundred miles, but with power steering, a comparatively little guy can run with the best of them—and win. In fact, in today's NASCAR, being smaller gives your team an advantage—the lighter the driver, the more options your team has in distributing a car's overall weight.

And there's no contesting that Jeff's looks appeal to the new generation of NASCAR fans. NASCAR has gone out of its way to create a "family values" atmosphere at the raceways. Christian chapel services for drivers and teams are held on race day at the tracks. Women abound. (When a new track opened up in Texas in 1997, the ownership put in twice as many female bathrooms as male.) There's still a Budweiser-sponsored car, but you can also see a Family Channel car and the Cartoon Network car—with Fred Flintstone on the hood—not to mention the Skittles and Cheerios cars.

Love him or hate him, Gordon has put paying customers in the seats at the speedways, people who would never have watched NASCAR even ten years ago. Because every Winston Cup race is now nationally televised, new enthusiasts are being drawn to the sport. John A. Krol, CEO of DuPont (Jeff's sponsor), says, "My mother-in-law is eighty-three and she's become [Jeff's] greatest fan. She's never even had a driver's license, and now she watches every race. It's incredible!"

Jeff's popularity is seen in souvenir sales, where he narrowly trails just one other driver—Dale Earnhardt—in total revenues. Chris Williams of Action Performance (which markets NASCAR-related products) explains why. "The trend with Jeff is a lot more with the kids and the ladies. His appearance means a lot, and kids like the color of his car, the rainbow color, and he's young. I mean, he likes video games and things like that. Kids can relate to him."

"Young" is almost an understatement. In the NASCAR world, where most drivers are in their thirties and forties (and several are in their fifties), Gordon is still freakishly young. Consider this: After driving six full seasons, Jeff was still the youngest of all Winston Cup drivers who raced every weekend. A trading card company opted to print a card of Jeff playing pinball rather than sitting behind the wheel of his number 24 car.

ESPN cable has credited Jeff with making NASCAR broadcasts profitable. John Wildhack, senior vice president of programming at ESPN, told journalist Robert Hagstrom, "We saw a big jump in 1995 because of the excitement centering around Jeff Gordon and Dale Earnhardt." That jump has carried through the late 1990s. On July 3, 1998, CBS TV carried the first (non cable) "prime time" showing of a NASCAR Winston Cup race on a network channel.

Jeff brought a jolt of adrenaline to a sport whose heroes were often old enough to become grandpas. After eight years of number 24 and the Hendrick Motorsports domination, one thing is clear: NASCAR will never be the same.

This is the story behind the young man who made it all happen.

chapter 2

Paying His Dues

> *"I don't think that when people are born, the doctor smacks 'em on the ass and a little sign rolls up on their forehead that says 'Race-car Driver.' People become products of their environment."*
> —John Bickford Sr. (Jeff Gordon's stepfather), 1997

Not too many five-year-old kids spend a Saturday waiting patiently while some adults lift a car that has landed on your shoulder after a wreck, but for Jeff Gordon, it was just another weekend in Vallejo, California.

Because Jeff began racing so young and succeeded so early, many fans mistakenly think he has not paid his dues. "Gordon is a spoiled little boy who never had anything go wrong in his life," said one. "What's he ever done, except win?"

In fact, Gordon has "paid his dues." He just began paying them about twenty years sooner than most other drivers.

Jeff's mom insists, "The people who say Jeff hasn't paid his dues, well, they don't have a clue. That's all he's ever done."

Two-Wheel Terror

Jeff had a need for speed long before he was able to control it. An early biographer, Mark Stewart, in his book *Jeff Gordon* (1996), quotes the star racer as saying, "I rode my first bicycle when I was two and a half or three years old.

I remember those days. We had a big hill at our house, and I used to ride down that hill on my bike, skateboard, roller skates—whatever I had."

Jeff's mom told me that her son started out directly on a two-wheel bike—no tricycle for him. He was younger than most boys in his neighborhood, so he learned that if he wanted to keep up, he couldn't putt around; he'd have to get used to going fast.

Not only was Gordon younger, but he was also unusually small, even for his age. At one point, his parents became truly concerned because Jeff just didn't seem to be growing. They took him to the doctor before he entered kindergarten, afraid he'd be picked on by the other kids since he was so much smaller. But the opposite actually happened. "All the little kids in the neighborhood thought he was adorable," Carol remembers. "He was just this little kid. Like a little baby to them."

The doctor didn't find anything wrong with Jeff. He just pointed to Carol and said, "Well, Carol, look at you. You're not very big!"

Because Jeff was so small, his stepfather, John Bickford Sr., had to customize his bikes just so that Jeff could reach the pedals. Ironically, this would make young neighborhood kids envy Jeff's bikes as much as grown men would one day envy Gordon's number 24 car.

"John had to customize the bikes so everything Jeff had was really 'trick stuff,' as John used to call them," Carol remembers, "so all the kids used to envy Jeff for that."

Bickford—who steered young Jeff into a racing career—entered Gordon's life early on. Jeff had just passed his first birthday when John took Jeff, Kim, and Jeff's mom, Carol, to a modified speedway race on Labor Day weekend in 1972. It was John and Carol's first official date—and Jeff's first brush with unbridled speed.

John and Carol had met while working together at a hospital-sickroom supply company. John modified vehicles for the severely handicapped; she worked in the front office doing billing. They were in their twenties with plenty of life ahead of them.

John admired Carol because he saw her as a "survivor." "She had two little kids in diapers," he recalled to me in 1998, sitting in his office, "and in those days they didn't have disposable diapers. Battling with two small kids, and laundry to do and no money." John found Carol attractive (anyone would—she has retained her beauty even today) and started coming by in the evenings to help her with the youngsters.

Carol was drawn to John's character: "He was a very caring person and extremely intelligent. He wasn't selfish and didn't think about what was right for him, but about what was best for [Kim and Jeff]."

When Jeff and Kim had finally been put in bed, the adults passed hours talking about what direction they wanted their lives to take. John is a man who is focused on the future, virtually consumed with the idea that a life is something you make, not something you inherit or wait to have happen. He raised Jeff with the belief that it takes absolute determination to get ahead—you set goals, then you chase after them with everything you have. The concept of "building a life" is clearly something that he enjoys contemplating, and something that, obviously, Carol wanted to become a part of.

Carol is reticent when talking about Jeff's biological father, simply saying that she had a "responsibility to not let the kids grow up" in "that kind of environment," adding that Will Gordon "now regrets a lot of what he did."

John, like Carol, had been through a divorce (and fathered one child—John Bickford Jr., who lived with his mother), but Carol found that rather than making John bitter, the experience had created compassion. "He took what could have been some very negative things in his life and turned them into something positive," Carol explains. "Not a lot of people do that."

John was an enthusiastic proponent of Jeff's fascination with motocross (BMX) bike races. He believed that if you use up as much of a kid's energy as you can doing constructive things, then the boy will naturally wear himself down and be tired enough at night to sleep. The bike track was just up the street from the Bickfords' house, so Jeff could go there with other neighborhood boys without his mom worrying about him.

With his characteristic passion, Bickford took Jeff out to practice bikeriding, watching his son ride so that he could figure out how to make the boy's bikes move faster. John's philosophy was indicative of the way Jeff would approach car racing. "What do I got to do to beat these guys?" Bickford told me he asked himself. "These guys are way bigger than Jeff, they're way stronger, and they're older [at four, Jeff was the youngest in his BMX age class], so what do I have to do to beat these guys?

"I got to be smarter. I have to build a lighter-weight bicycle. We'll have to practice more. Jeff has to beat the others off the start, and he'll have to have enough stamina to finish the race."

From early on, Bickford gave Jeff more than strategy. He sought to use competition to build the youngster's character.

"When Jeff was very young," Carol explains, "and kids would cut him off during a bicycle race, he'd be angry. John would say, 'Hey, Jeff, there's always the race tomorrow. Learn from this one and don't let that happen to you again.' John would never blame the other person with Jeff. He would always put the responsibility back on Jeff's shoulders.

"Later, when Jeff was driving cars and he came back from a race he might say, 'Did you see what that kid did to me? He cut me off!' John would respond, 'Why did you *let* him cut you off? *You* were the one who let that happen. Why did you put yourself in a position to let that happen to you?'"

In Bickford's mind, there's no such thing as bad luck. I pressed him on this once, asking him, "But what about when you do everything right and another driver still takes you out?"

"You didn't 'do everything right,'" Bickford responds in a deadpan voice. "You weren't fast enough to be out of the way. I don't believe in luck."

The intense focus paid off—Jeff actually won a bicycle motocross race when he was just four years old.

But Jeff's mother had her concerns. Her son was a "very small four," as Carol puts it, and most of the kids he was racing against were eight or older. "They looked after him on a Saturday morning," Carol says, "but during the races when they had five or six or as many as eight little bikes all lined up in a row, Jeff couldn't even reach the ground to be able to take off. The difference between four and eight is huge, physically and mentally.

"Jeff got up there and he would be this little itty-bitty tiny thing among all these huge kids and they'd take off and his legs would be pumping furiously, about ten times to every single pedal of the other kids. I turned to John and said, 'My goodness, this doesn't hardly seem right; he's pedaling ten times [faster than] them.'"

And then when they wrecked, "it was like dominoes," Carol recalls. Kids twice as heavy as Jeff piled on top of him, not to mention the sprockets, handlebars, and other bicycle paraphernalia.

"Watching the bigger guys race is what really scared me," Carol remembers. "They were hauling kids away with broken ribs in ambulances all the time."

Four-Wheel Five-Year-Old

Bickford responded to Carol's fears about BMX racing by bringing home two quarter-midget cars—a pink one for Jeff's sister Kim and a black one for Jeff. A quarter-midget is a small, open-wheeled car about six feet long, with a single-cylinder, 2.85-horsepower engine. There's a safety roll bar around the driver's cage, and its limited speed makes it a relatively safe ride for kids.

John did this without first consulting his wife. Carol was giving the children a bath when John said he had to "go pick up something."

A little later, after the kids were freshly bathed, John led Jeff and Kim outside and pointed to the two cars. Jeff's eyes were as big as saucers, but Carol's eyes narrowed.

"Oh, this is just great, John," she remembers saying. "We're going from bicycles to *cars*?"

Though Carol initially thought bringing home the cars "was a pretty crazy idea," she soon came around. "It didn't take me long to realize that it was much safer than what we were doing [racing BMX]."

Besides, as Carol remembers, "Jeff just took to it." She wasn't particularly crazy about her newly bathed son climbing into a car, but there was no stopping him. He just had to sit in it that night. John's fondness for racing no doubt had a strong influence on his young stepson, but he insists that he brought the cars home more as an experiment than anything else.

"It wasn't to push the kids into racing. I just wanted to give Jeff a chance to see if he liked it."

According to Carol, Jeff needed this guidance. "Jeff needed to be directed. He needed to have a lot of things to do."

Once it was clear that the boy was really into racing, John brought home a uniform, telling Jeff that if he looked, acted, and sounded like a professional racer, he'd be perceived as one. "From the day he was five years old, I approached it from a professional standpoint," Bickford remembers. "This wasn't about having fun. If we want to have fun, we'll go to Disney World."

An early picture of Jeff shows him in this uniform. His face is almost completely covered by the oversized helmet. He's number 55, and has GORDON written above the visor on his speckled helmet. He's wearing racing gloves, with a stripe running down the arm of his racing uniform. It's hard to imagine a five-year-old "professional," but if one could exist, he'd look a lot like Jeff in this photograph.

Now that Bickford had the cars, there was the problem of a track. There was an empty lot that hadn't been used in twenty years, just outside the Solano County Fairground. Men occasionally showed up to fly their model airplanes all around it, but that was about all the use it got. For Bickford's intentions, it was perfect. Though covered in weeds, underneath it was pavement. The asphalt had deteriorated, but it was good enough for a rudimentary track.

Bickford asked the fairground officials for permission to hack a small oval out of the weeds. The officials gave their approval, with the proviso that, of course, Jeff couldn't use the track during the fair or when any other event was going on. They didn't want people to be distracted from paying events.

That quickly was agreed to; John picked up a hoe, a rake, and a shovel, and measured off a 0.20-mile racetrack. He had purchased the *Quartermidgets of America Rule Book* and built the track to specification. Bickford doesn't do anything halfway. If it's worth doing, he does it right. That has always been his way.

Jeff often tagged along, helping as much as you can expect a five-year-old to help. It took three days, but finally a track took shape. Jeff jumped in his car and sped off, and wouldn't leave the car until the motor was too hot to run.

"We'd take that car out every night after I got home from work and run it lap after lap," Bickford remembers. "Jeff couldn't seem to get enough of it."

At first Gordon needed the practice. He was only five years old, after all, and even with a less than 3-horsepower engine to run on, "he slipped around that track for days getting use to the car and how to drive it."

It did not take long for Carol to realize there was something special about Jeff's devotion to that little car. Friends would bring their boys out to the track, expecting them to show the same interest as Jeff did, but often "they wouldn't have anything to do with it. They wanted to see it and watch Jeff, but those kids—many of whom were older than Jeff—were too afraid of it. No way were they going to get in that car," she remembers.

Even today, Carol wonders, "Why wasn't Jeff afraid of it? He wasn't afraid of the noise, of the speed; he wasn't afraid of anything. But all these other kids were petrified."

Grooming a Champion

I asked Bickford, "How do you teach a five-year-old to drive?"

"How do you teach a five-year-old to swim?" Bickford responds. "Or ride a bike? Jeff went out, drove around the track, spun around, and stalled the motor. I walked over to him, told him to try to keep the steering wheel straight until you get to the corner, and try to get your hands, feet, and eyes all working together."

Bickford took a laid-back approach. "What most parents do wrong is try to tell their kids too much," he says. "Kids have to experience things; they can't just be told.

"That's what I did different with Jeff than maybe other parents did. Instead of always telling him what to do, I listened and gave him the opportunity to comment. If I saw him doing something radically wrong, I'd bring it up, but it's often forgotten that kids have a greater desire to achieve than the parents have for the kids to achieve."

Kim, Jeff's sister, had no desire to race. She was in school when Jeff and Bickford carved out the track, but even when it was ready, it just did not hold much interest for her.

For his part, Jeff couldn't wait to test his skills against other drivers. Bickford and Carol agreed to let him race, but Bickford made sure the boy was ready. Jeff ran through *three to four thousand laps* before his first quarter-midget race. Bickford was concerned that Jeff not pick up bad habits, so before the eager youngster was allowed to start racing, Bickford forbade him from talking to other kid racers.

As always, Bickford was looking ahead. "When you got into the professional series of cars," he explains, "the norm is for all the drivers to run down and ask the guy who's going fast . . . what he's doing. Having been in racing a long time, I know you have to listen to your car talk to you about the way you drive the car. It doesn't matter what somebody else is doing or how they win a race, because it won't work for you."

The races were held on weekends, at established tracks all over California. Early on, John told Jeff, "Stay here in our pits. We'll do our thing and let our race car talk to us. When it talks to you on the track, you come back and tell me what it says. If it's saying, 'I'm pushing,' 'I can't turn the corner,' or 'it's too loose,' I'll keep adjusting the car."

This insular approach is tough, but Bickford believes it is essential for success. "What's toughest to teach kids is that there isn't any magic. There are no magic setups. There are no magic combinations. The only solution to success is hard work, and you got to stick with it."

Gordon's initial run was rather unremarkable, but fun. "I was having a ball, but I had a tendency to spin out a lot early in my quarter career. I didn't do that well in my first year of competition," Jeff remembers (keep in mind he was just five years old), "but I knew I could do it. Once I got it straight in my head how to do this stuff, I started winning, and the momentum just kept rolling."

That's an understatement.

chapter 3

Penske Prodigy

"We didn't go for a piece of the pie. We went for the whole damn pie and the crumbs on the table."

—John Bickford Sr., 1997

"The more I won, the more I wanted to race."

—Jeff Gordon, 1994

Soon Jeff's life was filled with racing. Several times a week he and Bickford practiced driving at the Solano County Fairgrounds. Just about every weekend, his family traveled to a race, often outside California. That left little time for church on Sunday (the Bickfords were usually out of town), or anything else, for that matter.

Jeff's greatest initial challenge as a five-year-old driver in 1976 was that, as the usual fast-time qualifier, he always had to start at the back of the pack. During the week, he practiced alone after school, and Bickford taught him to drive a lap faster than anybody his age. However, on the weekends during a race, he had to learn how to weave through traffic. This was harder to do.

On the way home, Gordon's familiar lament to his parents was, "I always get the fast-time ribbon, but I want that trophy." He'd usually pass most of the cars and gain the momentum, but the race would end before he had time to make it all the way up front. Second place became a cruel cliché.

That's partly why Carol became so involved in her son's training. "He needs to have somebody else out there," John told her, so they bought Carol a car and started simulating race conditions. Carol was small enough to ride in a regulation-size quarter-midget, though the seat had to be put back as far as possible. It would have been difficult for John to fit behind the wheel of a quarter-midget.

"We worked on [Jeff] setting me up to pass me," Carol recalls. "John would tell me what to do and I would try to do it. John was trying to teach Jeff where to pass, when to make the pass, and how to orchestrate the whole thing."

Once Carol got her own car, she started entering some of the moms' races. Kim came along to watch, but still had no interest in racing herself.

Carol says, "My daughter and I used to sit there, and when we first went, seeing the little kids was the cutest [thing] because they were all over the race-track; they were up and down, but there was Jeff, who had thousands of laps under him. He knew right where to run that car. He was not off and on the throttle; he was on the throttle, and 'Everybody else better get out of my way.'"

In case you're wondering, Carol readily admits, "Yes, he got black-flagged. [A black flag is waved at an individual car, telling a driver he has broken a rule and must get off the track.] There were times he got black-flagged for charging [being on the inside bumping through] and chopping [being on the outside cutting in]." At that age, in the novice class, black flags were learning tools more than anything else.

It wasn't just the racing that got into Jeff's blood—it was winning. "The more I won, the more I wanted to race," he recalls in a 1994 self-published autobiography, *An American Racing Fantasy*.

Maybe it was tactics such as the following that helped him get there. There's a well-reported early home movie of the young Jeff Gordon in action. At first, you can see a group of young boys driving calmly, all in line. Then, on the corner of the screen, a faster car takes over, just as the leader goes a bit wide into a turn. It's not wide enough to create a lane, but the young driver of the trailing but speeding car—Jeff, of course—makes a lane, literally running over the tire of the leader and then pulling into the lead and away from the field.

In 1977, five-year-old Jeff (he turned six that August) took home both the Western States Championship with the Baylands Quarter-midget Association in Sunnyvale, California, and the fast-time award with the Capital Quarter-midget Association. The next year, while other kids his age were reading books like *Dick and Jane,* Jeff won thirty-five main events—setting the fast time during every qualifying heat, and placing his name beside no less than five track records.

"We didn't go for a piece of the pie," Bickford reminisced to a *Details* magazine reporter in 1997. "We went for the whole damn pie and the crumbs on the table."

Tough Toddler

Jeff showed his toughness early on. A 1978 photograph shows Jeff driving number 97. A car behind him is sailing up with just one wheel on the ground. The right front wheel is literally resting on young Jeff's shoulder.

That same year, Gordon and two of his best racing buddies, Jimmy Gerrado and Paul McMahan, got into a particularly scary accident. Jimmy's two side wheels got caught up on Jeff's car. When Jeff's car kept moving, Jimmy's car flipped sideways. Jimmy was harnessed in the car, and the angle at which he was resting on the pavement made it difficult for him to get air. Jeff stopped racing and lifted Jimmy's head so that his friend could breathe until adult help arrived.

Jeff kept racing—and winning. It was considered unusual for a six-year-old boy to race year-round. Bickford remembers, "Most kids in quarter-midgets race maybe twenty weekends a year. We raced fifty-two weekends a year, somewhere in the United States. We had eight or nine cars. We practiced two or three times a week. We were perceived to be the Roger Penske of quarter-midgets." (Penske is a legendary racing-team owner. At that time, if you wanted to compliment a team's success, there was no higher compliment than comparing it with Penske.)

They certainly had Penske-esque success. In 1979, Bickford unleashed his prodigy on the national circuit, an organized series of quarter-midget races across the United States. Jeff tore through the competition, winning the Grand National Championship in Denver, Colorado. To prove it was not a fluke, he followed this success with fifty-two event wins, eight track records, and the Pacific Northwest Indoor Championship!

A 1979 family photograph shows Jeff in a yellow car after winning a light-modified-class race. One hand is on the steering wheel while the other carries a checkered flag. Gordon wears a red-and-black helmet with an imposing black visor. Not many kids can look menacing—especially one who is small for his age—but this one does, at least if you're behind the wheel of a competing car.

Gordon did not see his early success as anything particularly unusual. "It wasn't any special thing then because everybody was that young." But not everybody won so much.

In fact, the tracks soon started changing their rules. Just a few years earlier, five-year-old Jeff was complaining that he got the fast-time ribbons but never the trophies, because at that time only first-place winners got trophies. But Jeff started winning so much that most tracks started changing the rules, giving trophies to first-, second-, and third-place finishers. That way, other youngsters could have a chance to win a trophy.

"They made a lot of rules to get around things that we did," Carol told me.

Bickford's strategy was to move Jeff up through the classes as soon as possible, in part because he didn't want the boy to pick up the bad habits of each class. Family photos show how many and varied were the cars that Jeff drove in the early years. Since quarter-midgets aren't particularly expensive (around $2,000 at that time), Bickford was known to show up at a track with three or four cars—two for Jeff, and one or two for other kids he sometimes sponsored.

When people insinuated that Jeff won because of his car, Bickford went out of his way to offer moral support, even going so far as to sell Jeff's cars on the spot. "The car cost me $2,000 to build," Bickford often replied. "Give me $2,000 and it's yours."

Not infrequently, an eager dad would take up Bickford on his offer and watch in frustration as his son drove the new acquisition far less successfully.

Sometimes Jeff got upset when Bickford sold his cars. "I really liked that car," he would protest as the other boy's grinning dad pulled out his checkbook. Bickford calmed him down. "I'll build you another car that's even better," he promised.

The cycle would repeat. Bickford would build a new car, Jeff would run even faster, and another envious parent would approach Bickford. Soon that car would be sold. "Jeff would be upset with me again," Bickford admits.

But Bickford saw that the process actually built Jeff's reputation. Parents who had assumed Jeff won only because of Bickford's customized cars were silenced. "They realized that Jeff Gordon is a pretty good race-car driver," Bickford told me. "They'd put their kid in the car he just climbed out of, and their kid couldn't go anywhere near as fast as Jeff could. They learned to respect Jeff pretty quickly. He had a considerable amount of talent." Ironically, however, this charge—it's the car, it's the team, not the driver—would follow Jeff for virtually his entire career, right up to today.

Even more important than the actual driver training was the legacy of positive thinking that Bickford instilled in his son. "I try to think positive all the time. I look at every problem as an opportunity, because somebody's going to solve it—why can't that be me?"

This positive, can-do attitude presaged the attitude of another major influence on Jeff's life—a man who entered Gordon's life a decade and a half later. Race fans know him as Ray Evernham.

The Dominator

Eight-year-old Jeff Gordon dominated his racing class in 1980. He ran two cars and participated in over 150 races, by Bickford's estimate, and set seven track records in the process.

Jeff so dominated his home state (he won three California State Monza Championships) that he and Bickford continued to travel across the United States in a relentless pursuit of tougher competition. "I really felt comfortable and confident in those cars," the star racer remembers. "I felt that I could win just about every time out."

At that time, the California school system was based on a year-round schedule. Students attended school for nine weeks, then took three weeks off. During the off-time, Bickford packed the family trailer and took Jeff all over the country. Because John owned his own company (which manufactured products for handicapped people), he had a little more freedom of schedule than most people. Besides, Carol could run the business in his absence.

Jeff started boarding commercial flights alone as early as age eight. Because Jeff had to get back to school, there were several occasions when Bickford would drive the car and trailer home while Jeff caught a plane to make it back to Vallejo, California, in time for class. "You have to learn how to be a road warrior if you're ever going to be a racer," Bickford explains. "You have to learn how to travel and live on the road. It's not easy."

As soon as Jeff became comfortable, Bickford wanted him to face a new challenge. So in 1981, when Jeff was nine years old, he began racing go-carts. This made life even more hectic, as the boy was now racing two different kinds of cars.

At ten horsepower, go-carts have over three times the power of a quarter-midget. They are usually driven by fifteen- to seventeen-year-old kids, so as a nine-year-old Gordon was unusually small to tackle the appreciably larger tracks and higher speeds.

Jeff remembers, "With the carts, the tracks were bigger and the speeds a lot higher. When I started with the carts, I really had to work hard because the other drivers were tough [not to mention several years older] and they didn't want some newcomer coming and winning."

Maybe not, but they had to get used to it. Jeff won twenty-five of twenty-five dirt go-cart events that he entered in his first year.

Jeff still drove the quarter-midgets and posted a Region 4 Monza Championship in Indianapolis and another Pacific Northwest QMA win in Portland, Oregon.

Bickford had Jeff race less in 1982, but he entered him in bigger events. Jeff claimed the California State Monza Series and the Light "B" Class at the Grand National Championship.

Because of Gordon's small size and young age, his success looked almost freakish—a phenomenon he has faced his entire life. "All the other parents were saying Jeff was probably lying about his age, that he was probably twenty and just real little," Bickford told *Sports Illustrated*'s Ed Hinton.

"Nobody wanted to race us. That was fine. We moved up to the junior class, and he still kicked everybody's ass. These kids were thirteen to seventeen, and he was killing them. We then moved up to superstock light. Now we were running against seventeen and older—unlimited age. We were still winning. And those guys were going, 'There's no damn nine-year-old kid gonna run with us! Get outta here!'"

It sounds remarkable, but it's true. By age nine, Jeff was indeed routinely beating seventeen-year-olds. By the time 1983 had passed, Jeff had scored a total of four California Monza championships and two national championships in quarter-midgets as well as a growing number of cart wins. "We won every dirt midget race we entered," Bickford recalls.

And that's when Gordon hit a mental wall. Virtually his entire life was wrapped up in racing. Outside of video games, he had few other interests, and winning was becoming almost a certainty. The young racer was so successful, he was becoming bored. He needed a new challenge, and his dad was able to find it.

chapter 4

Sprints

"Being with the kids is all I did. I never did nothing but spend time with the kids. I had no recreation, no hobby of my own. Every day was spent helping the kids become what they wanted."

—John Bickford Sr., 1998

"Get out of here. I'm not going to build a sprinter for a child."

—Sprint-car builder Lee Osborne, 1984

In the mid-1980s, regional and state racing events became virtual locks—if Jeff entered, he almost always won, and everybody else raced for second. "By 1984, we were bored of quarter-midget racing," Bickford explains. "We were winning, had been doing it for too long, and it just wasn't fun anymore."

The relative ease of Jeff's early-on success blunted the boy's appetite for chalking up victories. It's hard to imagine someone being bored with success when they're barely an adolescent, but that's what Gordon was. The challenge was gone. "You get to be twelve years old, and you realize you've been in quarter-midgets for eight years," Jeff detailed to *Sports Illustrated*'s Ed Hinton in 1995. "What's next? I was getting older, not knowing what I wanted to do next."

Jeff's parents became concerned. The boy was winning so much that "he wasn't learning any more," Carol explains. John told Carol, "He's not learning, he's teaching, and he's way too young to be a teacher."

Carol adds, "Jeff needed to move on to the next level, but his age would not let him do that. So we thought, 'We'll buy him a boat.'"

When Bickford suggested Jeff try water-skiing, Jeff took to the aquatic sport with characteristic passion. Just as Jeff skipped tricycles for bikes, so he skipped using two skis for one. According to Jeff's mom, he got up on one ski—*the first time he tried.* As far as she knows, he's never been on two.

While this feat seems incredible, Bickford was not surprised. "John says that Jeff's hand-eye coordination is so above normal," Carol points out. "John picked up on that when Jeff was just five or six years old, watching him play Nintendo. He could play those things for hours and he was so good at it. There wasn't anybody that could beat him."

Jeff never stopped racing cars completely, but as he got more interested in water-skiing, he raced cars a few times a month instead of a few times each week. For a while, Bickford took Jeff out on the water just about every other day. When Gordon's skills improved beyond Bickford's ability to coach him ("The kid was unbelievable as a water-skier," Bickford says), he enrolled Jeff in two different water-skiing schools.

Where did Bickford find the time? "[Being with the children] is all I did. I never did nothing but spend time with the kids. I had no recreation, no hobby of my own. Every day was spent helping the kids become what they wanted."

Another obvious question is where Bickford found the money. Though hardworking, he was not a wealthy man. He was solidly middle-class, and his kids' events weren't cheap, so what he lacked in cash flow, he made up for with strict money management. Sometimes, he got unusually creative. "I made removable ski decks for the place that sold the boats, so he gave me Jeff's ski school for free. The other school cost me four or five hundred dollars, so how expensive is that? If you don't go out drinking, and you don't smoke cigarettes, and you don't go partying, and all you do is put your resources into the kids, there is going to be three or four hundred extra dollars laying around."

Jeff's personality was such that when he got into something, he wanted to conquer it, and water-skiing was no different. At the urging of his ski-school instructors, Gordon seriously considered turning pro, until he found a new racing challenge—sprint cars.

Much to the delight of future NASCAR fans, Bickford sold the boat in 1984 and Jeff never looked back.

Sprint Cars

It seems pretty bizarre, putting a thirteen-year-old boy behind a car designed to be driven by a full-grown man. However, Bickford was never one to let the unusual crimp his plans.

The move into sprint cars was never surprising—just its timing. For years Jeff had followed his heroes—Steve Kinser, perhaps the best sprint-car racer ever, Jack Hewitt, and Doug Wolfgang, just to name a few—by watching many of the track races live. Jeff proudly wore a Kinser T-shirt and followed the sport as closely as many of his fans now follow him. Everybody expected that Gordon would follow his heroes into sprints—after he grew a few more inches and gained several more pounds, that is. The average sprint-car driver was a professional in his thirties or forties, and Jeff was barely an adolescent.

The move into sprints received a boost when Bickford and Jeff perused a magazine article at a local store one day. The article told the story of a young man, not much older than Jeff, who had begun driving the more powerful sprint cars. Immediately their interest was piqued.

"I read everything I could about [sprint-cars] in *Open Wheel* magazine," Jeff remembers in his autobiography. "Then, too, many times after we were through racing quarters, we'd stop and watch the sprint-car races."

Never one to do things halfway, Bickford and Jeff flew to Indianapolis, Indiana, the undisputed capital of sprint-car racing, to get a closer look. At first, it seemed risky. Jeff had dominated kids driving 2.85-horsepower quarter-midgets and 10-horsepower go-carts—but putting a thirteen-year-old behind the wheel of a 650-horsepower sprint car? The idea seemed ludicrous. There were a few more logical steps—Jeff could have driven the full-up midgets, for instance. Sprint cars was a big leap, and the sprint-car world was horrified.

A sprint car can go from 0 to 60 mph in less than three seconds. Some can reach 100 mph faster than a Chevrolet Camaro can reach 60 mph (sprint cars top out at over 135 mph). During a race, the drivers use every bit of speed they can extract from their car, making sprint racing dangerous for a thirteen-year-old.

Though Jeff was sobered by the sprints' size and power, Bickford knew what his son was capable of, and he did not have any problem imagining Jeff behind the wheel of a near 700-horsepower engine.

Others did. When Bickford first approached a friend, Lee Osborne, who built and sold sprint cars (and had a son Jeff's age), about purchasing one, Osborne said, "Aren't you a little old to be starting out in one of these cars?"

Bickford maintained a straight face and replied, "It's not for me; it's for Jeff."

"I practically had to wipe him off the wall," Bickford recalls. "He said something like, 'Get out of here. I'm not going to build a sprinter for a child.'"

Bickford finally got Osborne to relent, though there were a few tricks that had to be figured out, such as designing a seat that was small enough for an undersized thirteen-year-old. "You know, Jeff wasn't what you would consider a normal-sized sprint-car driver at the time," Bickford quips.

Bickford took Jeff out on a lonely, California mountain road, and the teenager climbed behind the wheel. The road had to be lonely, as Jeff, at thirteen, was still three years away from being old enough to earn a driver's license and the car wasn't exactly street-legal. Since Jeff was prohibited from racing in California without a license, his practice experience behind the wheel of the sprint car was limited to this one shot. Stepfather and son knew they'd have to go out of state to race.

Many promoters, track owners, and insurance-company executives were adamantly opposed to putting such a young kid behind the wheel of such a big car. Bickford didn't expect to change everyone's minds overnight, but he noticed that the Florida All-Star series—a stretch of organized sprint races in Florida—did not list a minimum-age requirement. Bickford called the organizers and got the go-ahead. So in February of 1985 he and Jeff loaded their new sprint car into a trailer and drove across the country to enter Jeff in his first sprint-car race.

Jeff was cautiously optimistic about his prospects for racing. "I knew it was going to be tough," he remembers on his Internet Web site, "but all I wanted was the chance to prove whether I could or couldn't drive these cars."

Jeff and his stepdad arrived at the Jacksonville, Florida, track and started unloading the sprint car off its trailer. "People were looking at us like we were crazy when they found out I was the driver," Jeff remembers. The whispers reached officials and Bert Emick, who ran the All-Star series, sauntered over to Bickford's trailer.

"Who's driving the car?" he asked.

"Jeff," Bickford replied.

"No way!" Emick said it with a vehement finality. Not on his shift. Not when he saw how small a thirteen-year-old Jeff really was.

"You already agreed he could run," Bickford reminded him.

Bickford is not an easy man to say no to if one of his children's dreams is involved. Bickford may be patient and even somewhat gentle, but he is dogged. And he reminded Emick that based on Emick's previous words, he and Jeff had traveled a good three thousand miles.

Emick finally relented, but the whispers continued unabated. Bickford was even accused of child abuse, and these whispers reached the young Jeff's ears. Jeff became emphatic, insisting that racing sprint cars was something *he* wanted to do.

"There was *no* pressure from my stepdad about the sprint car," he wrote later. "Dad told me whatever I wanted to do, he would support me. I owe him everything and I do mean everything regarding my racing career. I would have been out there pleading for a ride, and at my age, I certainly wouldn't have gotten it."

Gordon adds, "I know he took a tremendous amount of criticism for allowing me to race, and I owe him a great deal for taking all that heat. If he hadn't stayed with me, I certainly wouldn't be where I am today."

With Emick's permission reluctantly granted, Jeff eagerly looked forward to his first sprint-car race at the All-Star Florida Speedweek in Jacksonville. If Jeff had known what humiliation awaited him, however, he might have thought twice about entering.

Racing a Boyhood Hero

Jeff sat behind the wheel of his sprint car and waited for the green light—
which would signal the beginning of his debut sprint-car trial run on a
real track against professional competition—to flash. After the start light
changed color, for perhaps the first time in his life, Gordon was stunned
on the racetrack. Cars didn't slide by him—they looked like they were flying. He quickly realized that he hadn't just entered a new level of racing;
he was in a new galaxy.

In his autobiography, Jeff describes the experience in his own words: "I
was idling around the track when they threw the green light and suddenly
these guys were flying by me like rockets . . . I was scared to death."

Jeff jumped on the gas—and went directly toward the outside wall of the
track! It was raining, the track was greasy, and it was an understandable mistake. Fortunately, his car just rubbed the wall and didn't do any damage to
the vehicle, but no doubt some of the officials were thinking, I told you so.

Gordon rolled into the pits, discouraged and disappointed. "I don't
think I can race sprint cars," he admitted to Bickford. However, then he got
a heavenly break—literally. It started raining, the race was canceled, and his
first professional mistake was buried by the weather. "It gave me a chance to
settle down before we went to the East Bay Speedway in Tampa," he
remembers.

Jeff didn't immediately dominate sprints at all like he had dominated
quarter-midgets and go-carts. However, he had multiple second-place finishes—pretty impressive considering sprint racing can attract middle-aged,
professional drivers. Even so, Jeff's racing was respectable enough to draw
the attention of the ESPN sports cable network, which ran a profile of the
unusually young sprint driver.

Bickford wasn't at all concerned that Jeff wasn't racking up first-place
wins. He was thinking long-term more than he was thinking immediate
dominance. The new cars gave Jeff a fresh challenge, and Bickford wanted
to build Jeff by having him race on different tracks (Jeff drove on twelve different tracks in his first year of sprint-car competition) so that he could
become a more versatile driver instead of a slave to one particular layout.

Each track has its own feel, its own grooves, and its own "character." Some drivers stay with one track and learn it so well that they can compete with the best, but on that track alone. If they got on a different track, they'd be crushed.

Rather than build Jeff's confidence in one arena, Bickford wanted his stepson to get wide exposure. Bickford was willing to lead Jeff away from immediate and almost certain victory to improve Jeff's skills in the long run. "We were there not to win; we were there to learn," Bickford explains. "We were fortunate to win a lot of races, but we were there to learn." It was a strategy that would pay off big-time in the long term, helping to make Jeff the dominant racer that he is today, winning on short tracks, superspeedways, and road courses.

Gordon's second season in 1986 (a racing season in sprints runs most of the year, from February through October) brought a lifetime highlight. At the Tampa Fairgrounds, Jeff actually found himself in front of the pack. Even more exciting for him, one of his pursuers was none other than his favorite racer, Steve Kinser. Jeff wasn't able to hold on to his lead, but managed a very respectable fourth-place finish. After the event, he got the compliment of a lifetime.

In his 1994 book, Jeff recalls, "After the race, I saw Steve Kinser walking toward me and thought, 'Oh boy, what did I do to him on the track?' He walked right up to me and said, 'Hey kid, you're going to be a good one.' Even today, I rate that as one of the highlights of my racing career."

Pittsboro

Jeff's second full season in the sprints—he was now fourteen years old—brought his first victory, at the KC Speedway in Chillicothe, Ohio, one of the few tracks that would let Jeff race. The drives to Florida and the Midwest were becoming tedious. This led Bickford to make some hard choices, including relocating the family from California to Pittsboro, Indiana. It was a small farm town with just one thousand residents, located about twenty miles west of the Indianapolis racetrack. Jeff and John moved there first; Carol and Kim arrived later in the year, in December of 1986.

The move was a major financial sacrifice. Though Gordon was able to earn a little money in his chosen sport, Bickford recalls that Jeff's earnings barely managed to pay the car's expenses, so living wasn't easy. "We had no money," Bickford confessed to one reporter, pointing out that sometimes they even had to borrow tires; at other times, Bickford worked on cars as barter. Bickford recounted in 1997 to a *Newsweek* reporter: "We slept in pickup trucks and made our own parts. That's why I think Jeff is misunderstood by people who think he was born to rich parents and had a silver spoon in his mouth."

Some people have reported that Jeff supported his family, but Bickford laughed at such a suggestion when I posed the question to him in 1998. "You could not make enough money racing with a youngster to support the cost of the racing. There was negative cash flow!"

When interviewing Bickford at his office across the street from the Charlotte Motor Speedway, I was struck by his willingness to literally bend his life around his children. In fact, many of the Bickfords' friends thought the move was foolish. "I've had people tell me they thought we were crazy for moving from California to Indiana," Carol recalls. "They probably don't think that now."

She pauses and laughs. "I thought we were a little nuts sometimes myself, especially in the wintertime. I hated the winters in Indiana. I used to tell John, 'I can't wait until we don't have to live in Indiana any more with those winters.'" (They now live near Charlotte, North Carolina.)

For John and Carol, the decision made perfect sense. Since it was undoubtedly best for Jeff's driving that they move to Indiana, that's all the reason they needed. "If we hadn't done it," Carol explains, "where do you think Jeff would be today?"

Jeff's options were far too limited in California. The tracks required him to have a valid driver's license to race sprint cars, and Jeff wasn't old enough to get one. A few states—including Indiana, but also Ohio, Michigan, and Minnesota—did not have this restriction. Moving to the Midwest was clearly the best move as far as Jeff's career was concerned.

But it never got easy. Many times, the Bickfords would cross state lines without any assurance that Jeff would be permitted to drive. It did not take

John long to discover that a verbal commitment over the phone didn't always mean that much once the officials saw how small Jeff was. Sometimes the teenager was even barred from a track after he had already competed there. Without clear-cut age guidelines, the issue of the boy's eligibility lay with the mood of local track officials.

Yet these disappointments, Bickford told me in 1998, helped make Jeff what he is today. "This kid has survived a huge amount of turmoil from different areas in his life. That's why he's so tough today. That's why he can handle situations that the average twenty-seven-year-old kid can't handle. He has always taken on big challenges in life; he's not one to hide from them."

Jeff welcomed his stepfather's single-minded drive. His entire childhood was focused on becoming the fastest driver around. The one time he questioned his desire to keep racing occurred when he was twelve years old. Bickford actively encouraged Jeff to explore other options. After trying other activities, the adolescent soon returned to driving. As he discovered from experimentation, racing was his destiny.

"In hindsight, I probably could've helped him win *and* have a little more childhood," Bickford acknowledges. "He could've been a very good saxophone player. His uncle was Elvis Presley's lead trumpeter. But it was never like, 'I want to play sax and you're making me race.' He wanted to race."

Jeff said as much when he talked to a *Details* reporter in 1997. "There's definitely some things we missed out on," he says, "but I don't think it's anything I could look back on now and wish I'd done. . . . Driving became a piece of me."

One thing was certain; if Jeff Gordon really wanted to become a professional racer, Bickford was prepared to make whatever sacrifice was necessary to give him that chance.

chapter 5

Fast Times

"I knew I wanted to race more than anything, but I never realized that it would end up being my career. I was living my life one day at a time and wasn't really thinking about what the future held for me."

—Jeff Gordon, 1994

Attending Tri-West High School was a "hectic time" for Jeff, according to his mom. "He'd get off school on Friday afternoons, get home, get in the truck, and we were ready to go. We were gone from Friday till early Monday morning. Often, Jeff had to sleep and do his homework in the truck. We'd go to Bloomington on Friday night; Chillicothe, Ohio on Saturday night; and back to Indiana on Sunday afternoon. I don't know how John did it, I truly don't."

Road trips and classroom studies took up most of Jeff's time during high school. There wasn't time for much else. He did compete on the school's cross-country team, and with his good friend, Todd Osborne, he'd shoot pool, try out the new video games, or ride around on skateboards. Jeff had girlfriends, but if they wanted to spend much time with him, they had to travel with Jeff's family on the weekends—and most of them did.

Jeff's school was small—his graduating class was less than a hundred—so it wasn't hard for teachers to keep track of what was going on. Though the majority of students knew their classmate raced, most didn't realize just how good he was, but Jeff was still popular, being voted king of the senior prom.

One of the series of races that kept Jeff so preoccupied during school was the World of Outlaws series. The WoO, as it's called, is a series of races established by sprint-car racers for sprint-car racers. It has a bit of a renegade reputation—racers taking things back into their own hands—but consistently draws the most talented participants in the world.

All this racing left little time for Jeff's studies, but fortunately, he found a teacher, Steve Williams, who shared his love of racing (and who, in fact, was a member of the local hot rod club in the Indianapolis area). Williams taught science, and, according to biographer George Mair (*Natural Born Winner: The Jeff Gordon Story*, 1998), the teacher and his pupil did much of their science projects and studies talking about racing and how an engine works, creating a friendship that continues to this day.

Though Gordon was a decent student, racing often came first, and he occasionally missed a Friday in class so that he could make it to a track in time for an evening race. It did not take long for Williams to figure out that Jeff's regular string of illnesses on Friday had more to do with four wheels and a finish line than with a coincidentally consistent string of viruses, so he'd often ask Gordon how the weekend race went.

Before long, Jeff settled down in his new home track of Bloomington Speedway. He got better and better, posting faster times and more impressive finishes—but even so, he still wasn't focused on a career in racing. Driving was more of a passion. "I knew I wanted to race more than anything, but I never realized that it would end up being my career," Gordon says on the history page of his Web site. "I was living my life one day at a time and wasn't really thinking about what the future held for me."

Gordon spent time in both the nonwinged and the winged United States Automobile Club (USAC) machines (two different forms of sprint cars); he drove on dirt, and he drove on pavement. If there was a steering wheel and four tires, Jeff was willing to give it a spin. Since many drivers don't even consider racing until they are well into their teens—and fewer still have parents willing to take them around the country in search of new driving experiences—it is hard to imagine any driver today having such diverse experience so early on, which helps to explain Gordon's phenomenal success.

Jeff began racking up a few track championships at Bloomington, then captured a title at the Eldora Speedway (in Rossburg, Ohio). He started racing internationally, in Australia and New Zealand, where he was sponsored by Australian car owner John Rae. Gordon literally dominated Down Under, capturing a stunning fourteen out of fifteen events entered and became well known in that part of the world. His wins came with style; he set track records at each one he visited.

Jeff came back to the United States in December of 1988. He tore through the competition, got his first USAC sprint victory at Florence, Kentucky, and proceeded to demolish numerous track records as he prepared for his high school graduation at Tri-West in late spring of 1989.

The Master of Midgets

Graduation night is usually a big party for most high school students; for Jeff, it was simply another chance to race at Bloomington Speedway in Indiana (he placed fourth).

After graduation, Gordon began racing full-time in a sprint car nicknamed *Beast*. Jeff continues using "B" names for his cars today. Ray Evernham (Jeff's Winston Cup crew chief) has said his all-time favorite Winston Cup car was named *Bob*. Unfortunately, *Bob* met a sorry demise during a practice run in Michigan in 1997 and was completely totaled. (Other cars Jeff has driven in NASCAR include *Blazer, Backdraft, Blacker, Butthead, Brooker,* and *Booger.*)

Beast was a well-used car. Consider just one short stretch in 1989: On May 20, Jeff won his first USAC sprint race in Florence, Kentucky; he raced in Haubstadt, Indiana, on June 3; Salem, Indiana, on June 11; Attica, Ohio, on June 16; Orrville, Ohio, on June 17; Kokomo, Ohio, on June 25; Indianapolis, Indiana, on June 29; Lawrenceburg, Indiana, on July 1; and Marne, Michigan, on July 3. These were just sprint races; this list does not count the midget races (which will be discussed shortly).

In 1990, Jeff notched a pair of third-place sprint finishes with four victories and three quick times in nine USAC races. ("Quick times" refer to preliminary laps run on a solo basis to determine the driver's starting position in the upcoming race.)

The USAC sprint series runs from early spring to late fall, with points given depending on how a driver does in any given race. At the end of the season, the driver with the highest points total wins the championship. Jeff was actually leading the series points race when he departed from it in midsummer to pursue other racing opportunities. Once again, he and Bickford were thinking long-term. They didn't care about a championship; they wanted new and varied experiences so that Jeff could continue to develop as a professional driver.

Among these "new and varied experiences" were midget cars, which Gordon began racing in 1989. Immediately, Jeff set track records and quickly began winning, eventually being named the 1989 USAC Midget Rookie of the Year. Jeff's success was not so surprising (for him), considering that midgets might be thought of as a "step down" from the sprints. "It was like going back to the quarter-midgets," Jeff remembers in *An American Racing Fantasy* (1994). "Like coming back home. I immediately felt confident with these cars. Today, they're still one of my favorites."

Gordon had an almost unbelievable weekend in May 1989. He set a new track qualifying record and took first place in his first midget race, then drove in three other open-wheeled cars—a USAC pavement sprinter, a Champ Dirt Car, and another dirt sprint car, all in the same weekend.

When Jeff dropped out of the sprint series in mid-1990 to concentrate almost exclusively on midgets (though he also ran a few dirt cars), his focus paid off with a midget national championship. At the age of nineteen, Jeff became the youngest person ever to win a USAC midget national title. Along the way, he garnered ten wins in thirty-five races.

Gordon's success was such that he started thinking about flirting with the most expensive and famous cars of all—Indianapolis cars. They're the open-wheeled cars that run in the Indy 500—they lie low on the ground and are the fastest race cars of all (other than dragsters). "Who knows," Jeff told the media in 1990 after successfully defending a midget race victory in Indianapolis. "Maybe in a couple of years down the road, I can get into an Indy car."

Thoughts of Indy were natural; after all, Jeff was doing so well with the Champ Dirt Cars, which are really just 1940-style open Indy cars. They're ten inches longer than the sprint cars but have a smaller engine and run a little slower than either sprints or midgets. Jeff was good enough to take the 1991 Dirt Car championship, posting two wins and two fourth-place finishes in a six-race series, and he became the youngest person to win the Silver Crown. Jeff had proven that there wasn't a mechanical horse he couldn't ride.

By this time, Gordon knew he needed to find a focus for his passion. Driving has become so diverse—from Indy cars to stock cars, even to pickup trucks—that eventually a driver has to settle on one choice if he wants to make a real living at it. Jeff has said to the media that he would have gone on to college if racing hadn't worked out. However, his success was an overwhelming incentive to continue driving professionally.

Jeff's racetrack achievements not only kept him out of college; they also ensured that suitors would come calling—the all-important sponsors who will pay for a driver's car in return for a portion of his earnings. In 1991, Toyota approached Gordon about driving one of their trucks. Jeff flew out to California to give it a try, then promptly rolled the truck three times and, in his words, "tore it to pieces."

"Boy, was I sore after that," he remembered in his 1994 autobiography. "I figured that my truck days were over, but [Toyota] still wanted to pursue it."

But Jeff wasn't so sure. John and Carol urged him to consider many options, including stock-car racing. They sent him to several professional driving schools and then offered to send him to a professional stock-car "academy" run by Buck Baker.

Jeff eagerly consented and flew out with his mom (he was still too young to rent a car and Bickford was tied up with business) to see what life was like inside a stock car. There was no question that the young man could race cars—but no one class or car had captured his heart to such an extent that he was willing to focus on that one vehicle for the rest of his professional life. He needed something he could focus on and stay committed to if he hoped to earn a decent living in the sport.

He found it on the North Carolina Motor Speedway.

chapter 6

The Birth of a Stock-Car Driver

"Well, Carol, Jeff's about to grow up real fast."
—John Bickford Sr., 1990

Carol Bickford, Jeff's mom, was about to get the ride of her life. She had come to North Carolina to let Jeff try his hand in a stock car, but she wasn't sure she was ready to drive in one—at least, not at speeds well over 100 mph.

Mother and son were at the stock-car academy run by Buck Baker. Baker is in the NASCAR Hall of Fame as a driver and today is the owner of the most prestigious stock-car driving school in the United States. His greatest claim to fame may well be turning Jeff Gordon into a devotee of stock-car racing. Once Jeff got a taste of asphalt and the heft of a stock car at Baker's driving school, he knew what he wanted to focus on for the rest of his racing career.

"The first day, the first time I got in a [stock] car, I said, 'This is it. This is what I want to do,'" he told *Sports Illustrated*'s Ed Hinton for the magazine's April 24, 1995, issue. "The car was different from anything that I was used to. It was so big and heavy. It felt very fast but very smooth. I loved it."

Sprint cars—which were the biggest vehicles Jeff had raced to date—weigh about a thousand pounds. Stock cars weigh 3,400 pounds. A sprint car is much smaller than a stock car, with room to seat just one person—

the driver. A stock car has roughly the same outward dimensions as many cars that are driven on the roads—the Chevy Monte Carlo, the Ford Taurus, the Pontiac Grand Prix, and the like.

After the second day of school, Jeff met Hugh Connerty, owner of the Outback Steakhouse car (professional stock cars are usually designated by their sponsors), which ran on the Busch Grand National Series, a professional level of racing in NASCAR just below the most elite series, the Winston Cup. (The Busch Grand National Series is the equivalent of the minor leagues in baseball or the Nike Tour in golf.) Connerty immediately perceived Gordon's talent and pumped Jeff up about stock cars and what they could do together if Gordon would commit to racing in the Busch series.

"It was an instant attraction," Jeff's mother, Carol, told me. "Jeff loved those stock cars. He was good at everything he did, but when he drove stock cars, there was something special."

Since Bickford was back in Indiana attending to his business, Jeff was eager to call his stepdad and let him know he had found his "calling." The young racer kept prodding Carol. "I've got to call John; I've got to call him. This is what I want to do for the rest of my life."

Carol tried to calm him down. "Jeff, hang on," she suggested. "Hang on." She wanted her son to take his time and work through this infatuation to make sure it would develop into a mature commitment. However, Jeff was so eager to tell John about his conversations with Connerty, Carol finally relented.

As soon as he got on the phone with Bickford, Jeff said, "Sell everything. We're going stock-car racing."

After Jeff was through talking, Carol got on the line. John listened to her talk about what had taken place over the past two days—including Hugh's promises—and John said, "Well, Carol, he's probably about to grow up real fast and find out what life is all about. Most of the time people promise you everything under the sun and they never deliver."

John was partly right; some of Hugh's promises never came true. Carol remembers, "Hugh Connerty wasn't able to do everything he said he wanted to do, but he did do a lot and he opened up a lot of doors for Jeff. That's where Ray Evernham [Gordon's current crew chief] came into the picture."

Before he left Baker's school, Jeff convinced his mother to accompany him on a practice run around the Rockingham track in North Carolina, where Baker's school is located.

"Just go slow," she pled with her son before the run. "I don't know if I'm going to like this."

Jeff hit the accelerator and took off. Carol realized Jeff wasn't a little boy racing quarter-midgets any more. "Jeff, slow down! Slow down!" she kept yelling.

"Mom, I am going slow," Jeff insisted. "The car won't go any slower."

First Break

Bickford's reservations about what Connerty could do for Jeff were understandable. In many ways, it's easier for a young athlete to participate in the Olympics than it is to get into NASCAR. To truly compete, you have to find an owner who is willing to invest hundreds of thousands of dollars in your ability to drive. Owning a stock car is a very expensive undertaking (top teams on the Winston Circuit spend several million dollars a year putting just one car on the track), and a good portion of that investment can be destroyed in mere seconds during a practice run if the driver does not know what he's doing.

But based on what he had seen at the driving school, Hugh Connerty decided to give Jeff a shot, signing him to close out the last three Busch races of the 1990 season. Connerty brought on Steve Barkdoll to help round out the team, and Barkdoll made the first call to a promising young crew chief named Ray Evernham.

Evernham listened patiently as Jeff was proclaimed to be the next big thing. He was skeptical, but decided to at least pay Gordon a visit in late September of 1990. He was surprised at how young Jeff looked, but the two clicked.

"They hit it off the first day," Bickford told me. "Sometimes two people just get along, you know?"

Jeff was "prepared" to get along with Ray, in that many of the qualities that mark Ray—confidence, high aspirations, high motivation—are reminiscent of Jeff's stepfather, John Bickford.

Carol remembers Jeff comparing Ray to Bickford by saying, "Gee, I just met my dad! I can't believe there's another John in the world."

It was a match, as they say, made in heaven.

"When we first started working together," Jeff told Mark Stewart, who wrote a children's biography of Jeff (*Jeff Gordon*) in 1996. "Ray impressed me, and I guess I impressed him. He impressed me because he had been a race-car driver. A lot of crew chiefs have never driven a race car, but Ray knew exactly what the car was doing."

In Gordon's recent autobiography, Ray points out the qualities that interested him in Jeff. "Jeff's intelligent and he listens to everything I have to say. He's quick to figure out the tracks and you only have to tell him things once."

It would be difficult to overestimate the importance of a good crew chief in stock-car racing. A chief has to make a lot of calls on behalf of the driver and will often direct and encourage the driver along the way. It's something that takes more than just "feel." It takes experience.

Evernham explained to journalist Robert Hagstrom, "Being a great crew chief . . . is [a] learned ability rather than just a natural thing, and that means you can do something to make yourself better."

One of Evernham's strengths is his incessant drive. Insiders close to him are amazed at how much time he devotes to his job. His single-minded devotion brings out the best in others as he encourages everyone around him to expect big things. "We are challenging at the highest level of auto racing in America," he told sportswriter Ed Hinton, "so why shouldn't we build an organization like the Yankees or the 49ers?"

Bumping in the Busch

The Busch Series races are usually shorter than Winston Cup events (300 miles instead of 500, for instance, though length of individual races varies from week to week, depending on the track). Also, they are held earlier in the weekend than their Winston Cup counterparts. The norm is for a Busch race to be run on Saturday with a Winston Cup competition on Sunday at the same track. Like the Winston Cup, the Busch season runs from mid-February to early November. Races take place all over the United States, from New Hampshire to California, with tracks in the Midwest and the South predominating.

In his initial Busch series race, Jeff got off to another colorful start. He crashed into the car manned by the son of his driving-school instructor. However, he drove well enough in the season's final three races to attract the attention of another owner, Bill Davis, who offered to sponsor Jeff for the entire season in 1991. Bill owned a car sponsored by Carolina Ford dealers.

Jeff is a goal-setter, and he aims high. He wanted to be Rookie of the Year in 1991 and claim the championship in 1992. Lofty ambitions indeed, and his initial forays on the stock-car track were less than spectacular. Just because you have a car does not mean you get to race. Each week, drivers must compete for one of forty-three spots, which are meted out according to an entrant's fastest time in two qualifying laps. Qualifying is usually held one or two days before the race. You drive two laps on your own, and your starting position is based on your fastest lap.

Jeff failed to even qualify for his first race, and it took another six events before he was able to break into the top-ten.

But once Gordon got the hang of it, he started placing higher and higher, including two second-place finishes, one third-place finish, and nine top-ten finishes—coming on strong enough to just inch out David Green for the Rookie of the Year award and claim $111,608 in prize money.

Meanwhile, Gordon was picking up accolades away from the track as well. This included the formation of the official Jeff Gordon Fan Club, which managed to sign up forty-seven members almost from the start. He was also voted on to the first squad of the 1991 American Auto Racing Writers and Broadcasters Association All-American Team. It must have been somewhat heady to share that honor with the best drivers in the world, including Mario Andretti and Dale Earnhardt.

But Jeff's sights were set higher for 1992: "I really think we have a realistic chance to win some races and challenge the championship," he predicted.

In 1992, Jeff's number 1 white car with red lettering (owned by Bill Davis) was sponsored by Baby Ruth candy bars. Though Gordon fell short of the championship, he certainly did challenge for it, ending up in fourth place. Even more importantly, he captured the attention of a team owner named Rick Hendrick.

History was about to be made.

chapter 7

A Sponsor's Dream

"What I found was a mature young guy who was kind of humble—a little bashful. A sponsor's dream."

—Team owner Rick Hendrick, 1992

It was March 1992 at the Atlanta 300 event in Atlanta, Georgia. The white Baby Ruth car half slid, half rolled into turn four. The young driver behind the wheel kept the car on line, but the executive watching him was certain that the driver could not keep racing a car that loose without running into disaster.

"Let's wait a minute and see this guy bust his tail," Rick Hendrick told a companion.

J. R. Hendrick III (everyone calls him Rick) is a wealthy man. And as the largest auto retailer in the United States, the man knows cars, so it was not too much of a surprise that he should be drawn to building a NASCAR dynasty.

Rick's life is full of highlights. In his early days, he was a minor-league baseball player; later he successfully brought a National Basketball Association (NBA) franchise to Charlotte, North Carolina, and for a time he held the world's fastest speedboat record. In 1992, when he met Jeff, he was forty-two years old.

Journalist Robert Hagstrom, in his book *The NASCAR Way* (1998), calls Hendrick "family fortunate": "From his father, a tobacco farmer, he learned how to repair engines. From his mother, a bank teller, he learned how to borrow money."

Put those two together and you have a potentially winning formula in NASCAR. Hendrick pioneered what he calls his "All-Star Racing Team" in the late 1980s. The norm in NASCAR at that time was for an owner to back just one driver. Though a few owners had attempted to sponsor several drivers, backing more than just one driver and crew had never been very successful. Hendrick was unique in wanting to integrate his drivers and crews to the extent that he did, getting them to work together, share information, and even, when the right situation presented itself, race together for each other's benefit.

The joint effort made sense. An owner could stretch out his research and development costs over three cars rather than one, giving him much greater spending power than the owner of a single car. Also, each car is allowed seven sessions a year in which the crew can take their vehicle on to a track to test it. Therefore, if an owner is working with three cars, he gains twenty-one sessions a year in which to perfect his cars' performance, provided the crews share information that is learned. Test time doesn't come cheap; when all expenses are considered, top-tier teams can expect to spend $150,000 per session, per car.

Hendrick told *Stock-Car Racing* (January 1997), "I related racing to the automobile business. . . . [By] being able to share information we were more successful. I could think of no reason why the same theory wouldn't work on NASCAR."

A visit to Hendrick Motorsports (just outside Charlotte, North Carolina) convinces you of one thing: Hendrick likes to work first-class. You won't find greasy floors and paunchy mechanics in this outfit. The floors shine and the mechanics wear snappy uniforms. Many of them hold advanced college degrees. When Hendrick decided he needed an aerodynamics expert, he recruited and then hired the top specialist from General Motors. Rick was the first to employ college-graduate engineers in every division to work on his cars. And it was his idea to train ex-football linemen for the heavy lifting required when working in the pits (a good jack man, for instance, must be strong enough to jack up a 3,400-pound car in one, single pump).

Hendrick zealously guards the domination he has created. Since NASCAR is forever passing new rules in its passionate pursuit of parity, team owners and engineers routinely spend hundreds of secretive and carefully guarded hours trying to find new ways to gain an edge. In a sport where two seconds is equivalent to a ten-run lead in baseball, minor adjustments are tremendously valuable. Just to be safe, Hendrick won't let any single person work on an entire engine lest his secrets be bought or revealed to another team.

Within just a few years, Hendrick's dream paid big dividends. His three drivers were all sponsored—by DuPont, Kellogg's, and Budweiser—giving him millions of dollars to employ over two hundred people who worked full-time with just one aim—getting one of their cars across the finish line a fraction of a second faster than anyone else's.

After four Winston Cup championships in four years, Hendrick's mastery is undisputed—in and out of the NASCAR world. (The Winston Cup championship is the top prize in the elite level of stock-car racing; it is determined via a points system that takes into account a driver's finish in every race during a single season.) When Hollywood wanted to pull off authenticity in the 1990 Tom Cruise big-screen movie, *Days of Thunder,* they knocked on Hendrick's door first to provide technical consultation.

Hendrick's dominance has reached such a high level that, as one journalist (Shaun Assael, in his book *Wide Open* [1998]) put it, "the chassis department at Hendrick Motorsports discards more cars than other teams build, and those rejects are so good that rival teams have begun inquiring whether they can buy them to race as new." How can a single driver-owner compete against an outfit like Hendrick's, which employs five engineers—research and design specialists—who work full-time and whose only job is figuring out ways to add a couple horsepower here and a couple horsepower there?

Even so, getting drivers to embrace such cooperation was not, at least initially, an easy sell in the tough-guy, independent-minded NASCAR world, and several early Hendrick drivers—including Geoff Bodine and

Darrell Waltrip—left to purchase their own teams. However, both Bickford and Jeff sensed that the future of NASCAR lay with Hendrick-type operations. Jeff explained to Hagstrom, "Rick was able to show every single person on his team that working together could pay off."

Back in 1992, Hendrick's vision of a dominant, cooperating stable of three cars was only that—a vision, not a reality. He needed to find drivers who could work together, which meant that he was on the prowl when he attended the Busch race in Atlanta in March of 1992.

Hendrick was walking to a luxury skybox—enclosed seats that have a sterling view of the racing-track compound—when his attention was drawn to one of the drivers on the track. He told *Sports Illustrated,* "I caught this white car out of the corner of my eye. As it went into the corner, I could see that it was extremely loose."

By "loose," Hendrick meant Gordon's car had a very dangerous chassis setup, which allowed it to go faster through the turns but made it harder to control. It was a gutsy car to drive, and showed a keen ambition and not a little confidence.

That's when Hendrick turned to his companions and said, "Let's wait a minute and see this guy bust his tail."

In 1993, Hendrick told Joseph Siano, a reporter for the *New York Times,* "Dale Earnhardt and Harry Gant were leading, and this white car was right up on them. I told the people with me, 'You just can't drive a car that loose.' But the car went on to win the race. I asked who the driver was. Somebody said, 'That's that kid Gordon.'"

Hendrick was overwhelmed with Gordon. "I was almost in a daze. Jeff had it all. It was just scary. He's good-looking, and I couldn't believe how well he handled himself at age twenty."

Another pleasant surprise was that though Jeff drove cocky, he didn't act that way. Instead of finding the prima donna that he expected, Hendrick told *Sports Illustrated* he was pleased that "what I found was a mature young guy who was kind of humble—a little bashful. A sponsor's dream."

Hendrick wasn't the only one interested in the Kid. Jack Roush and Junior Johnson—two well-known and well-respected owners—had made offers, as did legendary driver and now owner Cale Yarborough, who sent out some "feelers" to see if Jeff was interested in joining his team. Bickford told Yarborough in no uncertain terms that Jeff and crew chief Ray Evernham were a team; if Cale wanted one, he had to take both.

Yarborough balked and backed out.

Hendrick was clearly willing to bring out his checkbook for both Jeff and Ray, but Jeff was already spoken for. Gordon told Hendrick that he intended to stay with Bill Davis since Davis was trying to raise the necessary funds to start a team of his own.

With Hendrick's interest in his free-agent driver, Davis had more reason than ever to get sponsors on board, which he failed to do. When the money didn't come in, Jeff had a tough decision to make. "If there had been a Ford sponsorship in place, I would definitely have stayed with Bill Davis," Jeff insists in his autobiography.

The wise decision wasn't tough to figure out. Hendrick had deep pockets, and NASCAR was not a sport for paupers. The old days of an owner-driver were in as much peril as was the tobacco industry, which sponsors the Winston Cup championship.

"Bill Davis is a great guy and provided Jeff with a lot of opportunities," Bickford told me. "And he continues to be a great guy to this day. But what happened was that he and his team were without a sponsorship, and there was nothing on the horizon at the time. The opportunity presented itself with Hendrick, and all of the tools that it takes to be successful lay in Hendrick's toolbox."

What "tools" attracted Bickford? "You have to have resources, an organization, an engine department, team members, chassis, and all these things."

Within two months, in the fall of 1992, Hendrick had Gordon's signature and Gordon had Hendrick's backing. When a driver is signed, he usually receives a salary, and then turns over a portion of the money he wins to the owner. Typically, the driver keeps 50 to 60 percent, but this figure can be negotiated.

By leaving Davis and signing with Hendrick, Jeff Gordon, who had never won a Winston Cup race, was suddenly on the front page of almost every NASCAR publication. In handling the overnight media scrutiny, Jeff demonstrated a maturity and confidence far beyond his years. While he appreciated the opportunity Bill Davis and Ford had given him, he also remembered where he had come from. He hadn't been *given* a chance; he had *earned* it.

"Ford gave me a lot in terms of support and backing, but they didn't make me the racer that I am," Jeff points out in *An American Racing Fantasy.*

Davis was not happy about Jeff's departure—nor were many NASCAR fans. Gordon was surprised that leaving Davis created such a furor. The general consensus was that Jeff was abandoning the man who had given him his professional stock-car break. Others thought leaving Davis was just flat-out foolish. Jeff had the advantage of being the only man Davis was running; he'd be the third-stringer with Hendrick, and what kind of attention could he expect there?

Bickford provided the answer: "Rick Hendrick had all the correct tools and *the desire to win.* His personality is such that he wants to achieve great things. When you put people who want to achieve great things together, they usually achieve great things. The focus was on succeeding. They were not going to be distracted."

In his biography of Jeff, Mark Stewart quotes Gordon as saying, "I've never had so much negative response to anything I've ever done. . . . It was a tough decision, and I didn't know how it was going to turn out. But I felt that I was making the best decision for Jeff Gordon."

Over time, especially as Jeff Gordon became a dominating driver in the late 1990s, Davis got over his hurt and actually defended Jeff publicly when Gordon became one of the favorite drivers—both to love and to hate.

"[Jeff] gets a bum rap because he's a good guy," Davis has said. "He doesn't deserve the treatment he gets from a lot of people."

But you can tell Davis still smarts—at least a little. "You've got to be honest with how you feel," he told Skip Wood of *USA Today* (July 31, 1998). "And one side of me says he's a good guy and doesn't deserve the way he gets treated, and the other side of me says I think I'm a good guy and I don't deserve the way I got treated. That's just the facts."

To his credit, Jeff still feels a bit sad about the situation. "I've always wished success for Bill [Davis] because I saw how hurt he was when everything happened. It was hard for me to show him how difficult it was for me to make that decision, but sometimes you have to separate friendship and business. We talk, but I still see it there, the resentment of what happened."

In the wake of three championships in four years (with a second-place finish the other year), Bickford and Jeff's decision to go with Hendrick now seems brilliant. However, it took the forward-looking Bickford to fully grasp the potential of the Hendrick team concept back in 1992. "I've been in racing thirty-five years," Bickford told me in 1998. "I know that, guess what, next year the cars will be faster than they are this year. Five years from now, they'll be way faster. Don't tell anybody—that's a secret!" Bickford laughs. "I've been in this thing too long. If you want something to happen today, you better have done it a year ago."

Bickford and Jeff looked into the future of NASCAR, and they saw teams like Hendrick's, not Bill Davis' leading the way. Multicar teams, they believed, would outdistance the single-car teams.

And they were right.

It's worth pointing out that while Jeff took a chance on Hendrick, Hendrick also took a gamble on Jeff. In fact, Rick hesitated just slightly before signing Gordon's contract, thinking to himself, I have a daughter who's seventeen years old, and she looks older than him.

But both men proved willing to take a gamble that proved wildly successful beyond anyone's dreams.

Jeff joined veteran drivers Rudd and Ken Schrader on the Hendrick team. When Rudd left to start his own team shortly thereafter, Hendrick hired thirty-seven-year-old Terry Labonte to replace him. Jeff was just thirteen years old when Terry won his first (and at that time, only) Winston Cup championship in 1984.

Gordon's new Chevrolet DuPont Finishes car was first unveiled at the North Carolina Speedway in the fall of 1992. A crowd of fans watched as two men slowly pulled the brown canvas off a car unlike any that had ever driven NASCAR. The red rear melted into a yellow, green, then blue stripe. The blue flowed into a similar rainbow stripe up front.

A *rainbow*? In *NASCAR*? Jeff was gonna take a rainbow against leading tough-guy driver Dale Earnhardt (nicknamed "the Intimidator"), who drove a car fondly known as the number 3 *Black Bomb*?

But what a car number 24 would prove to be.

chapter 8

The Car and the Crew

"Let me put it this way. We're very comfortable with the return on our investment."

—Tom Speakman, marketing manager at DuPont Corporation, 1997

The intent of NASCAR is to place the focus on the driver, not the car. The idea is to have relatively similar vehicles so that the driver's skills, not the mechanics' wizardry, are put on display. The cars are modeled after current-year vehicles anyone can purchase off a car lot. NASCAR has approved six basic body types, including the Oldsmobile Cutlass Supreme, the Buick Regal, and the Mercury Cougar. However, most of the teams use a Chevrolet Monte Carlo or a Ford Taurus (previously a Thunderbird); fewer still drive a Pontiac Grand Prix.

Following a particularly scary crash in 1987, NASCAR began requiring restrictor plates (a thin piece of metal placed on top of the carburetor) on superspeedways. The plates restrict airflow into the engine (from an opening the size of a grapefruit down to the size of a grape), which cuts horsepower from 700 to 400. This dropped qualifying speeds that had begun to top 210 miles per hour to a slightly more manageable speed in the 180s to 190s.

Restrictor-plate racing also created a slight advantage for drivers of Gordon's stature, until new rule changes were passed in 1997. Jeff Gordon weighs about 160 pounds. A driver who might weigh 210 pounds drives a car with identical horsepower. You do the math.

Since 1997, teams are required to calculate the driver's weight (up to 200 pounds) as they prepare the car for a minimum weight of 3,400 pounds. Teams such as Gordon's still have an advantage, as they can choose where to put the extra weight. Teams with a 200-pound driver don't have a choice—it all goes behind the wheel.

NASCAR rules dictate the basics, including the chassis and engine displacement. Successful crews have to dig deep into the finer points of engine building and fine-tuning to create an edge for their drivers.

Hendrick Motorsports doesn't leave anything to chance, choosing to personally engineer every part that goes into one of its cars. Hendrick bought $4 million worth of equipment so that his team could manufacture their own parts. Jeff's custom-designed oil pan, for instance, costs $1,400. Factory-made oil pans for most cars cost less than $90.

The Fleet

Many casual fans may not realize that Gordon's Monte Carlo "car" is one of a fleet of look-alikes that are built and rebuilt specifically, according to the track Jeff will be racing on. His team maintains two short-track cars, two cars built for superspeedways, two designed for road races, and several intermediate cars for tracks from 0.5 miles to 1.5 miles in length.

The multihued cars have only two basic colors—orange and blue. Every other color is the result of immaculately placed decals. The "headlights," like the rainbow, are merely adhesive stickers that *look* like headlights. You never need car-powered lighting in NASCAR as most races are run during the day. For the few night races, lighting is provided on the track.

The unique features of the cars result from racing's demands. Jeff's seat is hand built from aluminum, and custom-fitted for his body. It is surrounded by a sturdy cage of steel rods. This cage helps to explain why an entire car can be demolished on the track and the driver escapes unharmed. With just one passenger, the entire car's protection is focused on that one section.

In his book, *Portrait of a Champion* (1998), Jeff mentions how he handles the psychological risk of racing cars: "This is a job. You can't worry too much about the dangers. And when you've done it as much as I have, you start to get used to the speeds."

I listened to Ray Evernham, Jeff's crew chief, tape a video for a DuPont product in September 1998 at the Hendrick compound in Charlotte, North Carolina. Evernham talked about the continuing quest to build a safer car. "Every time we have an accident or something happens to that car, we try to make it better and better and better."

Even though Evernham works with one of the best drivers in the sport, too much is going on during a Winston Cup race to ensure that his vehicle won't be wrecked. "You don't control totally whether you'll be in an accident," Ray said. "Other people are involved."

In fact, he added, "There's *going* to be an accident, but nobody says you have to get hurt in it." Virtually every Winston Cup driver gets in about half a dozen wrecks a year.

Ray's concern extends beyond Jeff to his entire crew. It's at his insistence that all "in front of the wall" pit crew members wear fire uniforms. ("In front of the wall" refers to those seven crew members who are actually allowed to work on a car during a pit stop. Pit areas are extremely small—in one stretch of track, officials have to provide room for forty-three cars—so the number of people allowed in front of the wall is closely regulated.)

"I don't want to be responsible for one of my guys having a scar," he explains.

One of the reasons Ray is so conscious of fire is that, as a driver, he was in one. It happened on October 31, 1982, during a modified race in Martinsville, Virginia. "Once you've felt that heat and felt the moisture go out of your mouth, you'll never forget that feeling," he says. "Fire is forever. If you break a bone, six weeks later, no one will know. But a fire scar lasts forever," he adds.

Since some of the pit crew members have "normal" workweek jobs—UPS drivers and the like—Ray is particularly conscious of their need to maintain their health. This in spite of the nature of pit stops, in which tragedy seems destined to take place.

"Seventeen seconds," Ray explains, "And in that time you're servicing the driver, changing four tires, adding twenty-two gallons of fuel—a fire can happen like that."

But more than to be safe, the car is specifically designed to go fast for long periods of time. The rear end of the car, as well as the transmission, engine, and power steering all have radiators. In addition, the engine oil tank uses a 110-volt heating blanket and plug-in heaters to keep the oil warm. You can see these special outlets on the cars if you get close enough to the vehicles.

Jeff can flip a switch that starts a fan that blows air though a piece of tubing into his helmet; this is called "the blower." Not only does it help keep Gordon cool during a race, but it also cuts down on carbon monoxide, which is pretty thick on a racetrack. The wind for the blower comes through a plastic scoop on the outside of the car, which captures fresh air. It is used to cool the oil tank as well as the driver.

For safety reasons, Gordon's car doesn't have a door; he slides in through a window, after which he puts up webbing (which will block most flying debris). His cockpit has ten switches with rubber extenders, making them easy to reach, and a large instrument panel for quick visualization. Some of the instrument readings are tilted sideways so that they are easier to see; when you're going 200 mph, you want to keep your eyes looking out the windshield.

One gauge Jeff does not have, ironically enough, is a speedometer. "Knowing my speed is a distraction; it just breaks my concentration," Gordon explained once. "I know when I'm running good or not, just by feel."

In case of an accident, Gordon has ready access to a "fire switch." One pull, and two nozzles will rapidly cover him with a fire-extinguishing and eventually life-saving spray.

Differing race conditions mean the car is constantly changing. During a 500-mile race, Gordon's car will go through up to five sets of tires. On an oval track, the right side will wear faster than the left. Along with changing the tires, the pit crew will clean out the front grille and air dam so that the engine doesn't overheat.

Gentlemen . . . Start Your Engines!

Nothing is easy about these customized cars—including turning them on. You and I need merely turn a key, but Gordon has to switch many levers in a precise order. He took Ed Hinton of *Sports Illustrated* through the process in 1997: "I hit my battery switch just a few seconds before I know they're going to give the 'start your engines.' Then I flip my tachometer on [a tachometer measures an engine's revolutions per minute], then my voltmeter [a voltmeter measures electrical force]. Then I hit the crank switch to get the engine turning. Finally I hit the start switch, which actually lights the distributor to give the power to start the engine."

Shifting isn't pedestrian, either. A driver has to be extremely careful when releasing the clutch of such a powerful car. "A normal passenger car has about 200 horsepower," Gordon explained to Hinton. "Even a Corvette has only about 300. We're talking 700-plus horsepower in my DuPont Monte Carlo. So it's really easy to spin the tires leaving the pit road. In a street car you have to get on the gas pretty hard just to get up to 55 or 65 mph. In my car I can do 65 in first gear and 100 easily in second, and I've still got two more gears to go."

Most often, the car is designed for running on a track, and since oval tracks exclusively turn to the left, Gordon has to constantly pull to the right on the straightaway.

"If you don't pull the car back to the right it will turn left on its own, because it's built to go through the turns as fast as possible," he explains. "I like a stiffer feel, so I can feel the front tires a lot more. But as a result, turning takes a lot more effort than it would in a street car."

Gordon also wants the springs and shock absorbers to be extremely stiff. "When you hit a bump in a race car, it's *'Uh-oh!'* It shocks you. But I want to feel the bumps so I know how the car's responding and can react to it. These cars actually ride better at full speed, as the banking of the track, the grip of the tires, the weight of the car, and the aerodynamic down-force compress the springs."

The high polish that you see on the car is more than cosmetic. The team works to get the smoothest finish possible to cut down on any possible wind resistance. No amount of resistance is considered too minor to take care of—that's why you'll often see Ray Evernham bending in front of the car, taping parts of the grille.

But a good driver and a good car are only part of a successful package. A champion also needs a good crew, beginning with an excellent chief. And Jeff has the best.

The Chief

Ray Evernham assembled and manages the DuPont team, often referred to as "the Rainbow Warriors." Evernham is a born motivator, pasting posters like "TEAM—Together Everyone Achieves More," "Refuse to Lose," and "God Made us Rainbows/Racing Made us Warriors" in his workshop.

I visited their garage, located just two miles from the Charlotte raceway, and saw the "Team 24 Checklist," which Ray unveiled in the team's first season:

From Nobody to Upstart
From Upstart to Contender
From Contender to Winner
From Winner to Champion
From Champion to Dynasty

Every goal has a checkmark next to it, except the last one. There's a check-mark nearby on a Post-it Note, however, just waiting to be moved into its proper place.

Another poster—this one signed by every member of the team—is located upstairs on the way to Ray's office: "The team that makes fewer mistakes will generally get the opportunity to win. The disciplined team has to get beaten by somebody; it refuses to beat itself. Rainbow Warriors: finding a way to win. 1998."

Downstairs is a posting of the "Warrior Creed":

Warriors hold themselves accountable. They expect warriors around them to bring it to their attention whenever they are misaligned with true north.

Warriors never quit. They know that they haven't failed until they quit.
Warriors are positive—not negative. They think about how they
will make it work versus why it won't work.
Warriors hate to lose! They know that friendly, honest competition
is fun and profitable.
Warriors say what they WILL DO. Then they do what they said
they would do—no fear, no failure, no excuses.
Warriors are happiest and most productive when surrounded by a
productive, positive environment. They know that they own creating that environment.

In 1992, Ray chose Andy Papathanassiou, a former collegiate offensive
lineman who holds a master's degree from Stanford University, to be his
number two man, and together they held tryouts to handpick the remaining Rainbow Warriors.

Back in the early 1990s, Evernham knew he was still on the learning
curve so he was cautious of hiring anyone who had a know-it-all attitude.
"We needed a group of people [who were] going to respect us, not people
who were trying to tell us how wrong we were all the time," he explained
to journalist Skip Wood in 1998. "If you want to start something new, and
if you have somebody who's been doing it for twenty years looking over
your shoulder all the time, all you're going to do is build a brand-new twenty-
year-old race team, and that's no good."

Fans cheer for Jeff Gordon, but he typically has at least forty and as
many as fifty people working behind him. During a typical race, there are
only seven who actually work on the car, and these elite few must be in
prime shape. If they struggle trying to lift a 70-pound tire or lack the bulk
to jack up one side of a 3,400-pound car in a single motion, they won't
make the cut.

A pit stop is an amazing thing to watch. Usually, four tires must be
changed and twenty-two gallons of gas must be dumped into the vehicle
while debris is cleaned off the car and the grille and air dam are cleared.
All of this needs to take place in no more than eighteen seconds if the team
wants to remain competitive (a single second in the pit stop forfeits about

three hundred feet on the racetrack). Every race is different, but you can plan on about ten pit stops per race, which means that the pit crew's actual worktime on race day is somewhere around two minutes—but it's a feverish two minutes!

Ray Evernham is known for his focus and a drive that propels him through many an eighteen-hour day. When I toured the Hendrick Motor Museum visitors stopped just to hear Ray talk about fire prevention. A worker at the museum explained why. "I'd listen to Ray talk about just anything," she said. "Ray makes you want to do a good job. He makes you want to be successful."

Being a Rainbow Warrior is hard work, with many of the full-time crew laboring seven days a week during intense racing stretches. Cars need to be built, and pit crews need to practice. The "early crew"—Ray Evernham and his closest assistants—log about seventy hours a week. The pit crew practices four hours a week, but puts in twelve to fourteen hours on race day. The shop crew contributes between forty-five to sixty hours a week.

In a sport where races can be decided in the blink of an eye, teams who ignore the importance of a quick and consistent pit stop do so at their own peril. "Pit crews can win or lose races for you," Evernham told *Sports Illustrated.* "So why shouldn't they receive as much attention as building a motor or a chassis?"

High-tech methods and systems prevail. Every pit stop during every race is captured on videotape by an overhead camera. These tapes are rewound and reviewed as team managers look for ways to save another precious half-second.

It's all very high-tech. *Popular Mechanics* (April 1996) raved about the $30,000 Pi Electronics package the Rainbow Warriors use, which includes a dashboard readout and four different communications, collection, telemetry, and analysis software programs. The magazine pointed out that the team utilizes twenty-eight channels of "analog data to monitor time, speed, distance, temperatures, pressures and flows, engine systems, shock travel, cornering loads, aerodynamics and other parameters."

When a race is going on, Evernham knows exactly what's happening inside Gordon's car.

Getting There

The valuable race cars are transported to tracks via a tractor-trailer rig. The fifty-foot rig averages about 40,000 miles per year traveling to races and test sessions around the United States. It is large enough to hold two separate race cars, as well as enough accessories to assemble several others: tires, tools, spare engines, a generator, and countless spare parts, as well as peripherals needed on race day, such as a roof platform for spotters and timers.

In addition to having a complete machine shop and welder, the trailer doubles as living quarters for a driver away from home. There's a kitchen, bathroom, and a room where Jeff can relax with a TV, VCR, and stereo system.

Add up the costs of three well-educated crews, the expense of building three fleets of cars, purchasing the trailers to transport them, and the expenses to keep everything running, and it's easy to see that stock-car racing isn't cheap. Ray Hendrick spends about $30 million annually to put three cars on the track—just under $8 million each, with about $7 million supporting joint research and development.

Much of the money for Jeff's car comes from his primary sponsor, DuPont. Though DuPont spends millions, they're far from reluctant about their financial commitment. It has proven very worthwhile. For example, in 1996, DuPont's sponsorship resulted in fourteen hours and fifteen seconds of national television exposure, worth an estimated $27.7 million.

Now let's track the history of this incredible racing team.

chapter 9

Rookie

"I'd like to think that someday, when people might think about me, they would say only one-hundredth of the nice things they say about Richard [Petty]. Even that's probably too much to ever expect!"

—Jeff Gordon, 1992

The NASCAR gods couldn't have planned it any better than this. Exit the undisputed all-time greatest Winston Cup driver ever, Richard Petty, in the same race that welcomes the young man—Jeff Gordon—with the greatest promise to unseat the legendary veteran who was now retiring.

The electricity at the Atlanta Motor Speedway for the Hooters 500 in November 1992 was higher than you'd find among a fraternity full of boys in the restaurant for which the race was named. It was the last race of the 1992 Winston Cup season, but the first Winston Cup race in Jeff's career.

I asked John Bickford if there was anything particularly exciting about this race, Jeff's first shot at the elite series. Bickford denied that either he or Jeff saw it as particularly momentous. To them it was merely the next logical step up the ladder, a ladder that Jeff and John had been climbing for almost twenty years.

"To people on the outside, they think of these as monstrous accomplishments, but to us it's just the next day of our lives. I don't congratulate somebody on the first day of their new job."

John and Jeff simply viewed the race as the next small step in Gordon's racing career. Both father and son had known this day would come and now it was finally here. There was no "Knute Rockne" type speech between father and son, no "you've finally made it to the big time and now we have to make it count."

"You just work hard every day, and when you work hard every day you don't think about [your first Winston Cup race] being a big deal," Bickford told me. "You test, practice, and work all year and you get into the car and have the best day you can possibly have. It doesn't matter whether it's a Busch race or the Winston Cup; you're just trying to do the best you can."

In practice runs, Gordon was determined to show he belonged—and he did, amazingly breaking the track record, clocking a scorching 181.31 mph. People were astonished that a rookie could come in and drive like that, but Jeff waved it off.

During qualifying, Jeff could have completed the fairy-tale beginning by taking the pole in his first race. The "pole" is the front starting position, given to the fastest qualifier. (Cars line up in rows, two abreast.) Jeff explained to the *Ragged Edge Race Report* (June 6, 1998) why the pole is such a coveted spot. "The pole does a lot more than you think. It gives you a good pit stall on pit road. It allows you to maybe set your own pace when they start the race and not have to worry about having to pass all those cars to get to the front and whether or not you're going to get caught in a wreck. I think all those things really help to put that car in contention to win the race by the end of the night."

Whether it was the nerves of having the time actually count or the awesomeness of finally being in the big leagues, Jeff's qualifying time was a full 3 mph slower than his best practice lap. It put him in the middle of the pack, twenty-first place.

The race itself was unspectacular. Jeff drove respectably, but cut a tire about halfway through, which took him out of the running with a thirty-first-place finish. Later that day Ricky Rudd—Jeff's teammate—had persistent problems with his power steering and became exhausted from driving his poorly handling car. According to NASCAR rules, drivers are allowed to use substitutes and since Jeff's car was out of the race, Rudd wanted to use his teammate, but NASCAR said no, calling Jeff "too young and too inexperienced" to serve as a stand-in. (Though substitute drivers are allowed, the points are always given to the driver who starts the race, regardless of who finishes it.)

Gordon's finish in thirty-first place earned him his first big-time paycheck: $6,285. Even more interesting, in the only race that Jeff and Richard Petty ran head-to-head, Jeff finished ahead of "the King" (Petty had an earlier accident and finished thirty-fifth).

It was inevitable that the press would make comparisons—a new driver in a new car, racing his first Winston Cup event during the King's last, but Jeff immediately put the kibosh on such speculation. "I don't think anyone can be another Richard Petty."

Little did he know that just a few years later, people might be saying, "Who would want Richard Petty's past when you could have Jeff Gordon's future?"

Getting Ready

Now that Jeff and his team knew 1993 would be all Winston Cup (no more "minor league" Busch races), they entered the new year with focus and intensity, exuding confidence. Rick Hendrick predicted, "I know it's hard for a young guy to come down here for the first time and jump into the ranks of talent that's Winston Cup racing, but I'm confident that Jeff will be able to win two or three poles in 1993, and if he can get up front, I think that you'll see signs of greatness."

But along with the predictions, Hendrick made it clear that he had no unrealistic expectations. He would give Jeff time to develop. "I fully expect him to make some mistakes this year and wreck a few cars," he said (not a small concession, considering the cost of replacing a car). "But I think that's the price you have to pay when you have a guy who's aggressive and has that kind of talent," he added.

Gordon started the season with three goals: He wanted to win at least one race, finish in the top-ten of the points standings, and be named Rookie of the Year.

A Win and a Kiss

By the time the "rookie" Jeff Gordon lined up for his first race in his first full Winston Cup season in February 1993, he had already won more than six hundred racing events. Even so, his car had to carry a "rookie stripe" on the rear fender. This stripe tells the other drivers who come up on a car that the driver in front of them is in his first season. When you're traveling 180 mph, you deserve to know how much experience the person has whose tires are a pencil length away from your own.

Dale Earnhardt, the dominant and most popular driver at the time—he shares the record number of seven Winston Cup championships with Richard Petty—decided to take Jeff under his wings (Earnhardt called him "the Kid"). Before the Daytona qualifier, during the practice laps, Earnhardt tried to simulate real racing conditions, and he worked with Jeff as the two drafted and passed each other, getting real close, just like it would be in a race.

"Drafting" is crucial, as the aerodynamics is such that two cars can go faster than a single car. Racing journalist Skip Wood asked Buddy Baker—who runs the school where Jeff learned to drive stock cars—to explain the concept of drafting. Baker did so for *USA Today* on October 8, 1998: "You've run across a paper bag on the interstate, and you look back and the bag actually comes toward the car," Baker explained. "That's because [the car] cuts a big hole in the air with the front end, and then the air going down the side splits.

"It starts to turbulate as it goes down the sides and over the top. When it gets to the back, it actually comes forward toward the race car, and that's what you call drag. So when a car behind you gets in this turbulence, it's actually pulling them toward the race car."

The way the cars are designed, drafting also allows you to make the car in front of you "loose" and hard to handle. It works like this. Engineers have figured out how to use the rear spoiler so that the wind coming off the hood of your car will create a down-force, keeping your rear tires firm on the track. This increased traction results in a faster car. When a vehicle comes up right behind you, it "steals your air" by taking the downdraft off your rear spoiler. On some tracks, this creates an effect that's not unlike driving on ice. Your car's rear end starts sliding all over the place.

Since Earnhardt spent considerable time with Jeff refining Gordon's familiarity with the mechanics of drafting and passing, reporters went up to him before the race and queried him about racing at high speeds with a rookie. Dale shrugged his shoulders. "I got no problem with it. [Jeff] doesn't move around on the racetrack and make dumb mistakes."

The real deal got started with the first race of the season. It was the Daytona qualifier. Since the Daytona is the first race of the season, they have leeway to make qualifying a more arduous, weeklong ordeal. Most races base qualifying on a two-lap solo sprint, held a day or two before the event. The Daytona 500 uses two 125-mile races to determine qualifying and starting position—though the pole is won the traditional way, by clocking the fastest of two solo laps. Jeff got off to a promising start. He became the first rookie in thirty years and the youngest driver ever (at twenty-one) to win the event. Jeff sounded like the kid he was as he chatted over the radio soon after he crossed the finish line.

"If you were on the radio, you would have heard a whole lot of scream-ing excitement," he told the media after the race. (Race fans can buy or rent scanners—what Jeff referred to as a "radio"—that allow them to tune in to each driver's frequency and listen to the radio conversation between a driver and his crew chief.)

Bickford was not surprised. "I'm never shocked," he told me. "You go to a race to win, and when you win, you say, 'Well, everybody did their job and that's why we won.' Everything fell into place per plan for Jeff Gordon for that first event. The plan was to move up very slowly, only pass when the opportunity presents itself, and that's exactly what he did."

The victory had a bit of a comedic ending. Earnhardt had taught Jeff a thing or two about drafting, but apparently he forgot to give him directions around the track. It seems young Jeff didn't know the way to victory lane! (Victory lane leads to a specially designated spot on the infield where win-ners are honored and awarded their trophy.)

"Never been there before," he laughed afterward.

It's a good thing Gordon eventually found victory lane because in this case there was a heck of a lot more than a wreath and a handshake waiting for him. The newly crowned Miss Winston, Brooke Sealey, was on hand with more than casual interest. As Miss Winston, she would get to kiss him in front of the entire racing world; but that one, very public kiss would soon blossom into a very private romance.

Daytona

NASCAR sort of does things backward in relation to the rest of the sports world. The Super Bowl and the World Series are played as the last contests of their respective seasons. However, NASCAR puts the most prestigious race—the Daytona 500—first. This can be done because the Winston Cup doesn't have one "championship" race. A championship is won by garnering points throughout the year. It is possible (and several drivers have done it) to wrap up a championship before the last competition is even held.

There are over thirty races a year (from mid-February to early November), with the vast majority of them run on Sunday afternoons. A few are held on Saturday. (Races postponed due to weather are usually run on Monday.) Every race counts equally toward a driver's end-of-season points count, but some races, because of their history and larger purses, are more prestigious than others, and Daytona leads them all.

Though Gordon had done extremely well to win the Daytona qualifying race, the intensity and length of the Daytona 500 would make it an altogether different contest.

What's so different? Most fans can't understand the steady, debilitating effect that driving a car at speeds rivaling 200 mph for several hours has on body and mind. It slowly but inexorably wears you down, particularly as you're working your way around a track with steep banks for five hundred miles. (A "bank" refers to the pitch of a curve on a racing oval, which ranges from a mild 9-degree bank at Indianapolis to a steep 36-degree bank at Bristol. On a 36-degree bank, the car will slide down the track if it is not going at least 90 mph. Road courses do not have banked curves.)

At any moment you are inches away from a spectacular crash. You have cars around you driving at speeds that carry a potent punishment for mistakes. Driving on the steep bank forces your head down at the same time that your body is strapped in place, requiring you to fight to keep your helmeted head up straight. Most people couldn't take the neck pressure alone after just three or four laps; added to that is the hellish, 150-degree furnace blast of heat inside the car.

And there's no let-up. In football, if you get tired you sit on the bench—but there's no "bench" during a NASCAR race. In basketball, if you need to use the bathroom, you rush in during halftime. There's no halftime in NASCAR. You're strapped into that car for the four or more hours it takes to complete the race. If something can't be done in seventeen seconds or less, you put it off until after the race is over. Winston Cup racing is one of the grimiest, hottest, most debilitating competitions out there.

As the 1993 Daytona 500 got under way, the fans were delighted, shocked, and thrilled when the Rainbow car started from the inside of the second row and immediately punched its way to the front. Jeff became the first rookie to ever lead the first lap of the Daytona 500!

Who was this kid?

Still, it was one thing to grab a quick lead. It was even one thing to win a short 125-miler. But what about when the cars started mixing it up for a 500-mile competition?

Jeff was well aware that as the bearer of a rookie stripe, he couldn't count on any veterans drafting with him if he pulled out of a line of cars to go for a pass. At Daytona, the track is fifty feet wide, allowing three cars to race abreast, but most often cars will run two-wide.

If Gordon tried to pass without drafting, he'd be buried. Two cars go faster than one, so if a driver slips out of the line of cars in front of him or behind him and no one goes with him, he is likely to drop half a dozen places in less time than it takes for someone to turn his head.

That's what Jeff knew he would have to avoid. His car was strong, but on a superspeedway a single car is still just a single car, so Jeff showed his maturity and sat patiently in line most of the day. When another car pulled out, Gordon jumped at the opportunity, but he knew his chances to create his own opportunities would be limited.

The strategy paid off. Anybody can lead a race for a lap early on. It's the end of a race that matters most, however; so as the Daytona 500 sped to another conclusion, spectators were jabbing each other in the ribs: *Look at that new Rainbow car! It's running in second place!*

One hundred laps earlier, second place could have been dismissed as a fluke. With just three laps to go, second place looked pretty serious.

It was NASCAR time.

Earnhardt was in the lead, and he must have had mixed feelings about having a rookie as his challenger. The good news was, Jeff might not have the experience to slip by him. The bad news was, could he control the car and not take Earnhardt out with a stupid move? ("Taking out" in NASCAR means crashing into someone and removing them from the race.) Earnhardt must have thought it was a little ironic that he had worked with just this driver, practicing the art of drafting and passing.

With just two laps to go, Jarrett challenged Gordon for second and won it. The cars bunched up going into the next turn. Jeff had to decide where to plow his field. He could follow behind Jarrett and possibly slip by Earnhardt, or stay behind Earnhardt and maybe retake second from Jarrett.

You don't have long to decide. Holes fill up faster than you can imagine when cars are hurtling around a track at 180 mph.

It made sense to follow the Intimidator (Earnhardt), and an educated guess is about all you get in such circumstances, so Jeff followed the black car . . .

He paid for it.

Jarrett punched forward and Geoff Bodine, in hot pursuit, blew by Jeff. Suddenly the Rainbow car was in fourth place.

Now everyone was fixed on the finish line—not just any finish line, but the Daytona 500 finish line. The final mad dash can be chaotic. The prestige and prize money of NASCAR's most important race is too great for manners. You just want to win.

Jeff had crossed hundreds of finish lines before, but never at this level and never against such competition. He held his own—but before the Rainbow colors flashed across the finish line, another car slipped by and Jeff went on to claim fifth in his first Daytona 500. Daytona is as big as they come in the NASCAR world; to run fifth in his first outing was outstanding.

No doubt Jeff really knew he had reached a new level when he was handed a six-figure check for his fifth-place finish—$111,000. Jeff had made more in a day than most twenty-one-year-olds will make in years.

Gordon's team was proud. Ray Evernham confidently told the media, "I don't think anybody really knows just how talented Jeff Gordon is. He doesn't even know that."

But there was a young woman who saw more than a little potential in Jeff Gordon. Her name was Brooke Sealey.

chapter 10

Love on the Victory Stand

"Look, you're young, you've got all this money, but you've never got any women around you. Are you gay?"

—Dale Earnhardt, 1993

Like Jeff Gordon, Brooke Sealey was also a sponsor's dream—in her case, R. J. Reynolds Tobacco—when it was announced she would be Miss Winston for 1993. Her resumé was impressive for a twenty-three-year-old. (She is one year older than Jeff.) Though she was a senior at the University of North Carolina at Charlotte (majoring in psychology with an emphasis on communications), and a fully pledged member of the Chi Omega sorority, Brooke was also a licensed insurance agent and a professional model. She had appeared in various promotional campaigns for Hanes, Chiquita, and Sony, and had won a regional spot promoting Diet Pepsi in the Carolinas. She was also a Miss North Carolina USA runner-up and a committed Christian.

A native of Winston-Salem, Brooke is a North Carolinian to the core. She was officially introduced as Miss Winston at North Wilkesboro in the fall of 1992, at a race in Charlotte. The 1993 NASCAR Winston Cup season was her first (and last) full campaign as Miss Winston.

Her requisite enthusiasm was perfect. "I watched with the rest of the world when Richard Petty ran the last race of his career at Atlanta Motor

Speedway [the previous year]," she told reporters. "I wanted to be there so bad. That was a special day, one that I will never forget."

Valentines

A friend of both Jeff and Brooke who worked for R. J. Reynolds made it somewhat of a personal mission to get the two of them together. He gave glowing reports of Jeff to Brooke, and equally stellar reports of Brooke to Jeff, but both were pretty busy and neither was that excited about blind dates.

And then the R. J. Reynolds representative showed Jeff a picture.

"I was impressed," Jeff recalls, "But a picture isn't the person. I had to meet her first."

The first face-to-face meeting was an official one—they both showed up to support a charity event put on by Rusty Wallace. Since both were there in working capacities, there was little room for romance to flourish.

"Those things are very hectic," Gordon confided to Terry Hoover of *Carolina Bride* magazine (January–March 1995), "so we just exchanged a few words. She was probably playing hard-to-get and I was trying to play it cool."

But now that Jeff had met "the person," he was more than a little interested. Several weeks later, they met again at a Winston Cup preview. Brooke was there as Miss Winston, and Jeff was signing autographs for fans. "Those autograph sessions are huge," Brooke remembers. "Thousands of people line up for autographs. But I brought him something from a young fan and asked him to autograph it. He invited me to sit next to him at the autograph table."

There wasn't much time for words, but Jeff was clearly smitten. "I was head over heels," he told Hoover.

Gordon phoned Brooke several times in early 1993, but he never got past her roommates. NASCAR rules stipulate that Miss Winstons are not allowed to date drivers, so Brooke opted not to call him back.

And then came Daytona 1993, which, incidentally, was held on Valentine's Day. Finally Jeff had a chance to talk with Brooke without going through her roommates. He approached Brooke when the two of them were in the garage area. According to Brooke, "He came up to me, and his little voice was just shaking. He was trying to talk to me, making the excuse that nobody else in racing was our age." Jeff doesn't have what you would call a deep voice, but it's definitely not squeaky, so obviously, he was nervous.

Brooke told one reporter, "He was so sweet—so down-to-earth. Actually, he was *not* down-to-earth. He was floating on a cloud."

Jeff took the opportunity to ask Brooke out to lunch on Monday. ("I never do anything on the Monday after a race," Gordon told *Carolina Bride*'s Hoover, "but I did that Monday.") His approach wasn't smooth, but it did the job.

"We got to talking," Brooke remembers, "and I found he was the sweetest person I'd ever met in my life. When he asked me out, he stuttered and stammered, but I said yes because he was so sweet about it—not cocky or arrogant at all."

Brooke handed Jeff a box of those message-laden heart-shaped Valentine candies for luck, and Jeff, no doubt riding a romantic high, won the 125-mile qualifier. Ever the sensitive sentimentalist, Jeff saved the candies instead of eating them.

After Gordon won the qualifier, he was whisked into victory lane, and Brooke's unadulterated attention. "I finally had something to talk to her about," he quipped to *Sports Illustrated*'s Ed Hinton in a 1995 article.

Miss Winston and the young driver started winking at each other in the victory circle. Brooke recalls, "We were all smiles and giddy. Nobody else knew, but we did."

A Secret Romance

The day after Daytona, the secret romance began in earnest. Though Jeff had driven five hundred miles the day before, he got into his car on Monday morning and drove the roughly one hundred miles from his home in the Charlotte area to Brooke's school in Greensboro, North Carolina.

He was still very nervous. "My palms sweat when I'm nervous," he confessed to Hoover, "and they were sweating like crazy that day because I knew right from the start. I'd never been with anyone like Brooke. It was hard for me to believe it was our first date. It seemed like the perfect match, like we'd been dating for a long time."

Jeff found something in Greensboro that he had lost in Charlotte—his anonymity. He and Brooke were able to date just like normal people without anybody from NASCAR finding out and causing trouble. They could go to movies, Japanese steak houses, and college parties, and not be bothered by autograph seekers. Pretty soon he was more than a visitor—he was a resident.

"When we first started going out, nobody at school recognized him," Brooke told *Carolina Bride*. "There weren't many race fans and Jeff had just moved here—so we could go to college parties and things. They treated him like a normal twenty-two-year-old. Because of his fame, he'd never been able to do the normal things kids our age do. We could just go out and be ourselves."

Jeff and Brooke's fondness for each other made both of them want to be together all the time. That meant the two had to learn how to duck NASCAR personnel. Thus began Brooke's odyssey of slithering out of public situations.

One time they were boarding a flight together when Darrell Waltrip's race team arrived at the same airport gate. Brooke slipped away and caught a later flight. On race weekends, Gordon became, in his own words, "a master at sneaking in and out of hotels." For her part, Brooke made a practice of checking out kitchen exits in a restaurant before she sat down with Jeff.

Gordon told his parents about Brooke early on, but made it clear that since Brooke was Miss Winston, the romance had to be kept an absolute secret. It was not until the March 1993 race in Atlanta that Carol, Jeff's mom, actually met her.

"They were paranoid," Carol told me. "Jeff didn't want anybody seeing his mom talk to her because he thought they might connect something."

Mom and future daughter-in-law actually met in the ladies' room at the Atlanta Motor Speedway. When Carol ran into Brooke, she immediately suspected that she was the one Jeff had told her about (there was more than one Miss Winston so Carol couldn't be absolutely sure on sight alone). Carol introduced herself. "You must be Brooke. I'm Jeff's mom."

The introduction had to be short. Later, a somewhat nervous Brooke told Jeff about the meeting, and Jeff got edgy. He called Carol and said, "Mom, you've got to be careful. Somebody could have been in there and heard you say that and probably would be wondering why you said that to her."

"These two kids were totally paranoid," Carol laughs. "It was a riot. We all used to get a big kick out of it."

Carol knew that Brooke was very special to her son. "Jeff had never been the type of kid to date a lot," Carol says. "When he dated, he dated one girl. When they broke up, he dated another girl, and they might go together a couple years. He was never one to date a bunch of girls—which made me very happy."

You can notice one change in Gordon—purportedly caused by Brooke—simply from the photographs: He lost his mustache, which he had been wearing since he was sixteen years old. Quite understandably, the racer had wanted to look a little older and thought the mustache helped. Brooke thought Jeff would look better without it. After they had been dating long enough for Brooke to feel like she could broach difficult subjects, she asked Jeff if he thought he would ever shave his upper lip. Shortly thereafter, Jeff excused himself, went into the bathroom, and reemerged sans mustache.

With Brooke secretly consuming so much of Jeff's affection, the other drivers began to wonder why Jeff showed such little public interest in women. This was red-blooded NASCAR after all. If Jeff wasn't drinking whiskey, at least he should be hanging out with the opposite sex.

But Brooke's Christian background, together with Jeff's participation in Motor Racing Outreach (MRO), a Christian ministry led by the Reverend Max Helton, was influencing Jeff to live an unusually "clean" life.

In 1998 Jeff told *New Man* magazine (March–April 1998), "Having God in my life has helped me considerably. I'm constantly growing in Him more and more. I'm trying to be more dedicated to God all the time. I'm still not 100 percent there, but I'm definitely taking the right steps. Brooke and I try to spend time together praying each day. Plus we have a Bible study with the Motor Racing Outreach."

Motor Racing Outreach organizes chapel services for drivers and their crews on Sunday mornings at the racetrack. Carol Bickford was somewhat surprised at Jeff's burgeoning religious interest. Though Jeff occasionally went to church as a boy, he was rarely home on Sunday so it was never a habit. However, Helton's and Brooke's combined influence encouraged Jeff to grow deeper in his Christian faith.

Gordon's lack of "womanizing" actually caused suspicion among some of the drivers. According to *Sports Illustrated* (April 24, 1995), Dale Earnhardt, not known for his sensitivity, finally cornered Jeff and said, "Look, you're young, you've got all this money, but you've never got any women around you. Are you gay?"

Apparently that's just Earnhardt's style. He likes to position himself as Gordon's opposite and rarely passes up an opportunity to get a laugh at Jeff's expense. In his book *Wheels: A Season on NASCAR's Winston Cup Circuit* (1997), Paul Hemphill writes that while appearing on David Letterman's late-night TV talk show, Earnhardt claimed to be the first man to win a NASCAR race at Indy. Letterman questioned him correctly, "I thought it was Gordon," to which Earnhardt replied, "No, I said I was the first *man*."

A Promising Start

The rest of 1993 was up and down—but more up than any rookie had a right to expect. A blown engine in Rockingham (North Carolina) took Jeff out early, but the next week in Richmond (Virginia) he managed a sixth-place finish. In March, at the Motorcraft 500 in Atlanta, Jeff qualified fourth and he drove like he intended to do more than place respectably. This kid drove to win.

"Driving to win" is not, by the way, something that every driver necessarily does. The points system favors consistently high finishes over first-place victories, so often you'll see a driver play it safe and race for a top-five or even a top-ten finish rather than risk crashing in the process.

Gordon led the Motorcraft 500 for over fifty laps, but his hard driving cost him. He was using too much fuel and had to make a stop for a quick splash. (Knowing how to conserve fuel is just as important as knowing how to go low or high to pass. "High" refers to the lane nearest the outside wall, where the track is raised on an oval; "low" refers to the lane close to the infield. These lanes aren't marked.) Obviously a driver cannot win on a tank that runs empty one lap before the finish line. Jeff went down a lap, but still salvaged a fourth-place finish. ("Going down a lap" means the leaders have gone around the oval one or more times than you have. If you're down one lap and pass the leaders, you're still behind them until you have completed as many laps as they have.)

Still, this was getting to be newsworthy: Four races, three top-ten finishes.

The next two weeks brought hard driving—and two crashes, but Jeff learned from each one and took another top-ten finish at Martinsville, Virginia, followed by two eleventh-place finishes at Talladega, Alabama, and Sonoma, California.

And then came Charlotte for the spring race (many tracks host two races a year—one in the spring, and one in the fall), where Jeff started in the middle of the pack and still finished second. He even led for a few laps but made a rookie's mistake and was penalized for jumping a restart. (After a caution flag is dropped due to a wreck or debris on the track, the cars slow down and wait for the restart. You cannot pass another car during a yellow flag, unless you come out of a pit stop ahead of it. A car is penalized if it gets ahead of the pace car or passes the car in front of it before the green flag drops, which begins the race anew at full speed.) Even so, he was able to come back and race for second place, then displayed fine racing maturity by holding on to second rather than blowing his position on a futile dive for first.

"We didn't have the car quite loose enough at the end to catch Earnhardt," Gordon told the media afterward. "I knew no one was going to catch me, so I just played it cool at the end."

As the 1993 season wore on, Gordon wasn't able to maintain the consistency he had shown in the first few races, but he had some spectacular showings, including second- and third-place finishes at the two races in Brooklyn, Michigan.

He also received his share of rookie "finger-pointing," on one occasion being publicly rebuked by veteran driver Darrell Waltrip, who accused Jeff of causing him to crash. Gordon's perspective was that Waltrip's criticism was unwarranted, but he was wise enough to let the matter die out quietly rather than start a public feud. Many a veteran has tried to foist his misfortune on to the rear stripe of a rookie.

With the racing schedule for the season more than half over, Jeff was still hanging on to a tenth-place position in the points race. That's a bit lower than he had enjoyed earlier in the year, but it was still a sterling effort for a rookie.

A Learning Season

There were a few good finishes in the latter half of the 1993 season, but also some disappointments, including crashes and repair problems.

Hopes were high for the fall race in Charlotte. Hendrick Motorsports is located less than two miles from the Charlotte Speedway. It was Gordon's new hometown, and as the season wore on, Jeff was eager to get the win he had set as a goal. The Charlotte race looked particularly promising after Jeff won the pole. He led the race for a lap, but that was about it, bringing home a fifth-place finish. Even so, winning the pole created a huge psychological boost.

After the high of the pole victory, Jeff's season ended on a disappointing stretch. A seventh-, ninth-, and fifteenth-place qualifying string led to three finishes out of the top twenty, dropping Jeff out of his goal of being in the top-ten in the points race. He finished fourteenth in the standings for the season.

All in all, 1993 was still a respectable year, the highlights being two second-place finishes. Jeff also began to develop that all-important consistency, with nine top-ten finishes, five of those being in the top five. It was enough to put him ahead of drivers with far more driving experience, but still kept him out of the top-ten in overall points standings. To be sure, his wallet was $765,168 thicker, and his showing was enough to get him elected Rookie of the Year.

By finishing in the top fifteen, Gordon had done more than simply drive with the best stock-car racers in the world. (There is no stock-car series that comes close to competing with the level of NASCAR; the best foreign stock-car drivers compete in the United States.) He had become one of them. Even so, he was disappointed that he had fallen short of his goals.

According to biographer Dick Brinster (*Jeff Gordon*, 1997), the racer reflected on his season by saying, "I felt like we were awful close to a win a few times. I just thought we'd win a race and one of our goals was to finish in the top-ten in the points. You like to reach your goals."

But he had won the respect of his fellow drivers—and the rookie stripe would come off. "That Gordon boy is a very good driver," Earnhardt said. "I have no problem racing with him anywhere on any track. He's probably going to win a lot of races and some championships."

In fact, a lot of fans started comparing him with the all-time greats, something with which both Evernham and Jeff felt uncomfortable. "I don't think it's fair to compare great drivers against each other," Evernham told Brinster. "Jeff doesn't like to be compared to other drivers. He doesn't like to be compared to Richard Petty or Davey Allison. It's not fair to Jeff or those guys. He's trying to be as humble as he can. He'll tell you he doesn't have a God-given talent. He'll tell you he's just driven race-cars all his life."

At the NASCAR awards banquet (it's always held in early December in New York City), Jeff was crowned Rookie of the Year, and Brooke's job as Miss Winston was officially over. The two did not wait long to take advantage of their freedom. They danced exclusively and closely, and everybody quickly got the picture.

Even with the building romance, Jeff's mind was still primarily focused on racing. "I knew there would be a lot to learn when I got to Winston Cup," Jeff reflected. "But the competition really is incredible. You can do everything right and still wind up fifth or sixth or twelfth because that many other guys are having a great race. But we do have a great owner and a great race team, and our goals are to be competitive, win some races next season, and eventually win the championship."

Gordon then said something that should have put the NASCAR world on notice: "I can't wait for next season to get started."

chapter 11

Slow Start, Fast Finish: 1994

*"[Jeff Gordon] was like any rookie. He's made mistakes in the
last year and a half, but there's not a guy in the garage who
doesn't think he has a lot—a lot—of raw talent."*

—NASCAR veteran Ernie Irvan, 1994

Carol was spending a quiet day at home in Charlotte, North Carolina,
when the phone rang, early in 1994.

"I need to talk to you and John," Jeff said.

Immediately Carol knew what he was going to say.

"So you want me to get John on the phone?" she asked coyly.

"Yeah," Jeff answered.

Carol found John Bickford in the shop and told him, "Jeff is on the
phone and he wants to talk to both of us."

John smiled. He knew what was coming, too, and when he and Carol
got on the phone, Jeff confirmed it.

He planned to ask Brooke to marry him.

A year to the day Jeff had first asked Brooke out, he reserved a place at
a French restaurant. Unfortunately, Unocal was having a major function
that night at the same eating establishment. Jeff didn't want any NASCAR
fans to be around when he asked Brooke the most important question of
his life, so he stalled. He visited the men's room frequently. He ordered
dessert. He waited until the Unocal crowd thinned out and left.

Finally he proposed, Brooke cried, and the engagement was settled.

The emotions of romance translated into a competitive spirit on the track. Jeff boldly told the media that his fiancée made him "a better driver." Well, he'd get his chance to prove it.

Clash Gordon

The year 1994 started with the Busch Clash (held at the Daytona track) in February, an all-star event of the previous season's pole winners plus one name pulled out of a hat. It consists of two ten-lap sprints (fifty miles total), with the initial starting positions chosen at random, by lottery. After the first break, the field is reversed so that the person who comes in last starts first.

Jeff began the race in sixth place; after the first run was over and the positions were swapped, he started the second run in fourth. With the veterans charging back up to the front, things got crowded and wild real fast. Veteran driver Ernie Irvan had to start from the back but methodically worked his way up front. Earnhardt and Brett Bodine charged after him, and Jeff decided to put his lot in with them, catching a very effective draft in the process.

Earnhardt took over the lead, while Jeff drove patiently behind Bodine. At just the right moment, Jeff caught a draft and catapulted himself into the lead, where he took the checkered flag. A few drivers looked at the kid and started talking about "Clash Gordon."

An engagement and a win. Not a bad way to start off the year.

Frustration

Jeff rolled into Richmond, Virginia, for the March 6, 1994, Pontiac Excitement after a fourth-place finish in the Daytona and a thirty-second-place finish in Rockingham, still hungry for his first points win. However, the NASCAR gods have ways of frustrating every driver, and on this day, they were clever. Jeff was running strong through much of the race when he noticed that something was seriously wrong as he drove out of a pit stop on lap 276. His left front wheel was detached and rolling free in front of him!

A few loose lug nuts could have spelled disaster, but, amazingly, the car sustained only sheet-metal damage, and the Rainbow Warriors pit crew were able to get Jeff back out in ninth place—this time, with four wheels intact.

Jeff drove hard enough that afternoon to garner a third-place finish, quite impressive considering the unexpected breakdown, but not quite as well as he had hoped.

Still, a win at the Busch clash and two top-five finishes aren't a bad way to start a year—unless they are followed by an eighth-place finish in Atlanta, a thirty-first-place disappointment at Darlington (North Carolina), and a string of races in which Jeff finished twenty-second, fifteenth, and thirty-third respectively.

The angst seemed destined to continue as Jeff looked ahead of him at the Winston Select 500 in May 1994. He barely qualified, in fortieth place out of forty-three available spots.

Much to the delight of Ray Evernham and team owner Rick Hendrick, Jeff weaved and bobbed, went low and high, picked the right drafts, and looked like he owned the field as he drove his way into first place. His first Winston Cup win was tantalizingly close. But Jeff got tangled up in an accident. He came out all right, but not before half the pack had passed him. He finished a disappointing twenty-fourth. On his way back to his trailer, Jeff knew he wasn't racing go-carts any more. Winning was no longer his middle name.

Gordon qualified much better at Sonoma (California)—sixth place—but still came in a discouraging thirty-seventh. That dropped him all the way back to eighteenth in the points standing for the season championship.

People started whispering. Maybe Jeff was not such a hot driver after all. Maybe Ray Evernham didn't have what it takes as a crew chief. Maybe Hendrick's vision of a three-car team simply wasn't feasible, as the owner's attention was spread too thin over three cars instead of one.

A Breakthrough in *Brooker*

The Rainbow Warriors hauled a car named *Brooker* (yes, it was named after Brooke, Jeff's fiancée) to the Coca-Cola 600 (Charlotte, North Carolina) in May 1994. During qualifying, *Brooker* felt strong and fast. Jeff knew he had won the coveted pole—the first-place starting position—before he hit turn three. "I was smiling all the way down the backstretch," he said.

But Gordon had qualified well before. For once, he needed to finish up front, and three-fourths of the way through the race, Jeff was in good shape. A caution flag gave the cars a chance to dash into the pits. Rusty Wallace came out first, followed by Dale Jarrett, who had led before the caution. The green flag (restarting the race) dropped on lap 324 of the four hundred laps total. (Every race has a different number of laps, depending on how long the track is—from half a mile to over two miles—and how long the race is—typically, from 400 to 600 miles.) By now Wallace looked like he owned the lead. Jeff was fighting for third behind Jarrett, with Bodine by his side.

On lap 370—just thirty laps to go—all the crew chiefs began going through their calculations. Every driver needed more fuel and new tires, but exactly when?

It's a gamble at this stage. If you pit too early and something happens on the track that brings out a caution flag, you can lose valuable position and get caught in the middle of the pack. It's preferable to pit during a caution because the cars are following a pace car traveling approximately 55 mph. That gives the cars an opportunity to pit and get out before any one car laps them. But if you run out of gas or are forced to drive a car with worn-out tires, you court disaster. Since nobody can see the future, there's far more art than science to choosing the right time to make a pit stop.

Wallace's crew opted to pit first, bringing him in for a stop nine laps later. The pit was picture-perfect, and Wallace came out fast—but not in the lead. Evernham kept Gordon on the track, mulling over a tough decision. In the early 1980s, Richard Petty had taken the checkered flag at the Daytona 500, in part by taking on just two new tires at the final pit. This allowed him to come out of the pits a few seconds faster.

"Two-tiring" is a risky strategy—and dangerous. One blown tire and more than the race can be lost—the driver's health is put at risk. And since cars with two new tires have less traction than cars with four new tires, they tend to have less speed and control. If you're going back out with tired tires, you better go out with a comfortable lead.

Despite the risk, Evernham thought the Kid might be able to pull it off. And they needed a win. Ray told his crew to go with two tires, and sent number 24 out of the pits 250 yards in front of Wallace.

Jeff won with a phenomenal 3.91-second victory.

His first Winston Cup win!

Jeff's dad, John Bickford, saw everything unfold from the track pits, but his mom Carol was up in a condo watching with two close friends, Steve and Linda, and two future in-laws—Brooke's mom and stepdad, Mr. and Mrs. Everett Glenn Parks Jr.

Since nobody thought Jeff could catch Wallace until Ray's brilliant call in the pits, everybody in the condo was shocked at what they had just seen.

"It was a madhouse," Carol recounted to me. The guy who owned the condo was trying to figure out how to take Jeff's family and friends to see him in victory lane, but after a race, everybody is moving in one direction—away from the track. Trying to get into the infield is pretty tough without a helicopter.

Linda had a headset on and was listening to Gordon's frequency. She turned around and faced Carol, who saw tears streaming down Linda's cheeks.

"What's the matter, Linda?" Carol asked.

"Jeff's crying, Carol," Linda said. "He's *crying.*"

That made Carol start crying. "It was pretty exciting," Carol remembers. Jeff was just a couple months shy of his twenty-third birthday. He had been racing for eighteen years, and every mile led up to this.

The entire world was privy to Jeff's tearful emotion. The television cameras caught him openly weeping as he sat in the driver's seat. When asked about it, Jeff even admitted to crying while driving: "I was trying not to hit the wall from all the tears that were coming down my face," he said.

In the Winner's Circle, Jeff proclaimed, "This is the happiest day of my life. This is a memory and feeling I'll never forget. If there's a feeling higher than this, I don't know what it is."

"You can't imagine how hard it is to get to this point," he added. "It's just wonderful; it just truly is."

Wonderful, but debilitating. Jeff was so exhausted he required oxygen to stabilize his breathing.

As Gordon was overwhelmed with happy emotions, his competitors were shaking their heads with surprise. Dick Brinster, a journalist and biographer (*Jeff Gordon,* 1997), recorded Gordon's stunned fellow drivers. "I'd have to say Gordon outfoxed everybody tonight," Jarrett said.

Wallace, who had led for almost half the race, felt the loss most keenly. "In hindsight, we should have changed two and we would have won by a ton. But it was a pretty savvy move on their part. They did a good job."

Bodine spoke more succinctly, but captured the feeling as well as anybody: "I can't believe it," he said.

After the race, Gordon received his first first-place NASCAR check. Most individuals in their early twenties never see a six-figure check—certainly not with their name on it. However, Jeff was slightly baffled about the $196,500 check. He thought the arbitrary number was a bit silly and good-naturedly suggested to the track owner, Bruton Smith, that he should make it a nice "round" figure.

Smith pulled out a wad of money that could have wallpapered a small room. He began counting out hundred-dollar bills, one at a time, until he got to thirty-five. *Now* Jeff had his round number—two hundred grand!

After the exhilaration of a big NASCAR win on May 29 came the reality of a grueling NASCAR season. There were two strong showings in Dover (Delaware) and Pocono (Pennsylvania)—a fifth- and a sixth-place finish respectively, but then a string of relative disappointments, with just two top-ten finishes (two eighths) in the next five events. It was enough, however, to work Jeff back into the top-ten in the points race, though he was still over 600 points behind the leader, Dale Earnhardt.

And then came the Inaugural Brickyard 400.

The Inaugural Brickyard 400

Back in 1982, when Jeff was eleven years old, he watched Rick Mears win the Indy 500. After the race, Jeff and his dad worked their way through the crowd to reach the infield, where Jeff waited for over two hours to get a T-shirt autographed by Mears. Bickford watched as the famous Indy racer took the time to talk to young Jeff. After Mears turned away, Jeff looked up at Bickford and said, "Someday, I'm going to race here."

Just a decade ago, racing at Indianapolis would have meant racing Indy cars (open-wheeled models that lie close to the ground). That's why Jeff thought his dream had died when he entered the Winston Cup: "It was a dream of mine to go race at the Indianapolis 500," Gordon wrote in his 1998 photo-essay book, "and when I went to NASCAR I thought my chances were gone."

A lot has changed since Jeff Gordon was eleven years old—not least of which has been NASCAR's phenomenal growth in popularity, which led to the inevitable marriage of Winston Cup racing at the hallowed ground of Indy, much to Jeff's delight. "When they announced the inaugural Brickyard 400 for 1994, I was ecstatic. I don't think I ever wanted something so badly than to win that inaugural."

Indy's estimated quarter million spectator seats were quickly sold out for the debut Brickyard. Curiously, track officials closed off the infield. No official explanation was given, leading some to speculate that perhaps officials were somewhat chagrined about having the first stock-car race draw more spectators than any Indy race had ever drawn.

Before the race, Jeff sounded like a kid at Christmas: "It's finally here. It's finally gonna happen . . . because it seemed like before . . . it was all rumors and a lot of hype and a lot of talk."

Even before practice began, Jeff started talking about the history of the event. "I lived about fifteen or twenty miles from here out in Hendricks County," he told reporters. "I went to Tri-West High School and graduated from there. To make history here in NASCAR is more than a dream come true. This is one of the greatest things I've ever done in my life. To see all these fans when you come driving down that front straightaway is just the greatest thrill ever."

Remember, this was said before Jeff had even *qualified.* But everybody could feel the excitement in the air.

The Rainbow Warriors worked on the car all week, fitting it out especially for the 2.5-mile oval track at Indy. They opted not to use *Brooker*, but instead went with a car affectionately called *Booger*.

During practice, Jeff was confident that *Booger* was a capable car. Later, during qualifying, Jeff finished third, and his confidence grew the next day during another practice run. "There wasn't anybody I couldn't run down," he said.

Gordon was particularly excited about this race because for once he'd be running on a track where he had no less experience than any other Winston Cup driver. "This [is] a track with no history of Winston Cup races," Jeff explained to Brinster. "It's tough to race on those tracks where all these guys have been racing for so many years. Right now, we're just learning the ropes, learning the racetracks."

At the pre-race drivers' meeting, Winston Cup director Gary Nelson pleaded with the competitors to drive carefully. Since this was the first Brickyard 400, he pointed out, it would be remembered as a historic event. "And you don't want your grandkids to point at your picture and say, 'My grandpa did something dumb at Indianapolis,'" Nelson quipped.

At least three drivers were not listening. On the very first lap, Dale Earnhardt managed to make contact twice—first with pole-sitter Rick Mast, and then with the wall in turn four. He came out of both altercations slightly bent out of shape but still charging.

A little later, the Bodine brothers (Geoff and Brett) took a family feud into the public arena, playing bumper cars through turns three and four. That dispute almost took out Jeff.

That's the tough part of Winston Cup driving. The fast-paced world of NASCAR requires more than skill. Most drivers will tell you it also requires a little luck, and Jeff seemed to have his share that day. First, he narrowly avoided a collision with Geoff Bodine as both cars raced into the pits. Later, Jeff would once again narrowly miss Geoff after Brett Bodine bumped his brother and sent him into a spin.

"That's when you know it's your day," Jeff told Joseph Siano of the *New York Times* (August 8, 1994) after the race, "when breaks like that happen."

Gordon's strong car exerted itself early on. Overall Jeff led ninety-three of 160 total laps. With about twenty-five laps to go, the race developed into a high-speed form of "bumper tag" as Jeff remained locked in a duel with Ernie Irvan. The two cars ran nose-to-tail.

It was looking like one of those basketball games where the team that had the last shot would win, and Jeff wasn't particularly thrilled that the guy with the last shot might be Irvan. "The last guy I wanted to race at the end was Ernie," he admitted later.

"It was a mind game," Irvan said of the classic duel. In staying so close to Jeff, Ernie was paying the young driver the classic compliment. You don't get in such a tight spot with a driver if you're not sure he can handle his car. "I had a lot of confidence in Jeff," Ernie allowed.

Finally Ray weighed in, urging Jeff to bide his time. "Wait for the word on when to pass Ernie," Ray said. Evernham opted to have Jeff drive side-to-side, counting on the fact that such side-to-side driving might help wear down Irvan's tires and give Jeff a chance to pull away at the very end.

On lap 156—just four laps to go—the Kid got more than he hoped for. The side-to-side punishment did more than wear down Ernie's tires; it punctured one. Irvan went wide, Jeff shot inside to take the lead, and Ernie had his hands full just trying to miss the wall. Ernie ended up in the pits, allowing Jeff to finish with a comfortable four-car-length margin over Brett Bodine.

The stress of actually pulling out the win, added to the elation of doing it before a hometown crowd, came together in another touching emotional display. Tears started streaming down Jeff's cheek, even before he crossed the finish line. He had to take an extra victory lap "to wipe away the tears."

"I can't control my emotions at a time like this," Jeff explained, "But I don't want to be known as a crybaby all the time."

Not exactly your normal NASCAR confession.

While Jeff was wiping away tears, Ray Evernham was shaking his head. "By God, we've got a great driver," Ray said, watching Jeff's car come in. "The Kid is just phenomenal."

In the winner's circle, Gordon was beaming, "This is the happiest day of my life." He said he felt like "a kid in a candy store."

Ernie gave accolades to the young driver who had just beaten him. "[Jeff Gordon] was like any rookie," Irvan told the media. "He's made mistakes in the last year and a half, but there's not a guy in the garage who doesn't think he has a lot—a lot—of raw talent. He's already done things at an age when most of us were not even sitting in a Winston Cup car. I know I'll be racing him most of my career."

The small-town boy had won big.

Gordon made it clear that though winning an historic race was nice, his sights were set even higher. "The topper of them all would be to win a Winston Cup championship," he said. "It may be out of reach this season, but we're the team of the future."

Instead of celebrating on the town with steak and champagne, Jeff and Brooke went back to their hotel room to watch a taped replay of the race. They ordered a pizza and were told that there would be a two-hour wait.

"How come?" Jeff asked.

"We're really busy because they just had a race over at that racetrack," the pizza man told Jeff.

Gordon was *really* hungry. "Does it help if I'm the winner of that race?" he asked.

There was a stunned silence on the end of the phone. "Uh, let me get the manager," the guy said.

Shortly, Jeff heard, "*Mr.* Gordon, may I help you?"

How do you like that. Mr. Gordon! And Jeff had just turned twenty-three two days earlier on August 4!

"Yeah, do you think it's possible to get a pizza in less than two hours?" Jeff asked.

"I think so," the manager replied. "We'll certainly see what we can do."

A hot pizza was delivered to Jeff's and Brooke's door about thirty minutes later. Winning does have its privileges.

For sure. Gordon had just won the biggest purse to date in NASCAR history—a $613,000 jackpot. However, with that jackpot came excruciating expectations. Jeff would learn that those that cheer the loudest often turn around and jeer you just as loud—all in less than twenty-four hours' time.

Expectations

Jeff couldn't sleep at all that night. He was still pumped up about the race and kept replaying it in his mind—the start, the passes, the head-to-head duel with Ernie Irvan. However, when he got out of bed the next morning he'd find that his dream win would help create his second public-relations nightmare.

The little farm town of Pittsboro had gone crazy when Gordon's car crossed the finish line in first place. West Main Street doesn't have much more than a dozen businesses, but virtually every one soaped its windows with a congratulatory message for the hometown conquering hero in anticipation of his expected visit.

But NASCAR had other plans. They asked Gordon to renege on a previous commitment to make an appearance at the Tri-County Speedway (near Pittsboro), insisting that the winner of the inaugural Brickyard go immediately to Disney World and serve as the grand marshal of a parade. As a sponsor, Disney had spent millions of dollars to help make the first Brickyard a success, and they were adamant—the winner had to be there.

When the local fans showed up at Tri-County for a celebratory breakfast fete and Jeff didn't, many people took it personally. Jeff tried to explain that it tore "his heart out" to miss the fan club gathering, but not everybody was mollified.

Gordon was fortunate to have Bickford on his side, who showed up at the Tri-County gathering with Carol. Every person was given the opportunity to cancel his/her breakfast reservation once Bickford explained that Jeff and Brooke were out-of-state. Most everyone stayed and was treated to a recording of Jeff finishing his last twenty laps of the Brickyard. The fans got to hear Ray and Jeff plot, strategize, and then celebrate. It wasn't the same as congratulating Jeff in person, but the hometown fans had to learn that Jeff was bigger than a local hero; he was on his way to becoming a national icon.

Breaking In

Jeff still had a dozen races to run in the 1994 season, out of which he garnered five top-ten finishes, including a second-place finish at the Miller

Genuine Draft 400 in Richmond and a fourth-place finish at the Slick Fifty 500 in Phoenix.

As the tires cooled after his last race of the year—his second full season as a Winston Cup series driver—Jeff had climbed into the top ten of the Winston Cup championship, finishing a strong eighth. From now on, he wouldn't be taken for granted, and his driving would be respected. He had broken into the big time.

You can not overestimate how important respect is for future racetrack success. Rick Vogelin, writing for *Sport* magazine (February 1995) explains, "Auto racing is a brutally competitive sport, and nice guys seldom finish at all. The initiation of a newcomer—even one with Gordon's credentials— can be a high-speed hazing that roots out the poseurs and pretenders. Racers are as ruthless as a wolf pack when they catch the scent of weakness."

Jeff had been tested but had come out all right. "There were times . . . when some guys would do a little extra just to test me and put the pressure on," Gordon told Vogelin. "You take it up to a point. Then you have to fight back."

Gordon wasn't the only member of the Rainbow Warriors winning peer respect that year. Ray Evernham was named Crew Chief of the Year. While 1993's disappointments and the early-season fiascoes in 1994 had created whispers about whether Ray had what it takes to help his driver win, the brilliant call at Concord (the Charlotte Motor Speedway is actually in Concord, North Carolina, but it's so close to Charlotte that the two cities are frequently named interchangeably when referring to the speedway), and Jeff's strong showing at the Brickyard had silenced the critics.

Winning has a way of doing that.

But Jeff's success in 1994 went beyond the track. He was about to lay claim to the biggest prize of his life.

chapter 12

Drafting on the Dance Floor

"Since [Jeff's] been married to Brooke he's a totally different person. He's more patient. I think she has really helped his driving."

—Ray Evernham, 1995

Now that the 1994 racing season was over, Jeff Gordon could focus on important personal matters: He and Brooke were scheduled to be married on November 26 at the First Baptist Church in Charlotte, North Carolina.

Picking the date had been the easy part. The NASCAR schedule doesn't give a driver many options. "Everybody in racing celebrates their anniversary during the same two weekends of the year," Brooke explained to Terry Hoover of *Carolina Bride.* "The [last two weekends of November] are the only two weekends during the season you can get married."

Planning the wedding was a little more difficult. Jeff and Brooke didn't want to be apart (during their entire engagement—from February 14 to the November 26 wedding day—they were separated for just two days), and since Jeff was in a different city virtually every weekend, Brooke had to engage in long-distance planning. She received much-needed help by hiring a professional wedding planner.

A traditional NASCAR-laden bachelor party can be a sorry sight and not something one might want to commit to print particularly. However, Brooke's influence on Jeff was already showing. He opted to forgo the traditional bachelor party route and instead participated in a giant paint-ball war. Rick Hendrick rented a facility in the Charlotte area for the party's private use, and Gordon's buddies, colleagues, and male members of his family stalked each other through the woods in a 1990s version of a very messy (and somewhat painful—those balls hurt when they hit you) tag.

The Saturday-evening wedding was, in Carol's words, "huge and beau-tiful. It was almost too big. There were so many people there I didn't even get to see, but it was beautiful; it was a gorgeous wedding."

Three hundred and fifty family members and friends convened at the First Baptist Church in Charlotte.

Jeff's celebrity status made preparations a bit difficult. He and Brooke had decided beforehand that though they would provide security, if a fan showed up who had gone to the expense of renting a tuxedo or buying a formal dress, they'd be accommodated and given a seat in the church bal-cony. But they set limits, too. "If they showed up in a Dale Earnhardt T-shirt," Brooke joked with a reporter, Terry Hoover, "they'd have been turned away!"

What the couple did not want was for the wedding and reception to evolve into an autograph-seeking haven.

Jeff asked his crew chief, Ray Evernham, to be his best man. Brooke's maid of honor was Alyson Stewart, a UNC college roommate and best friend since middle school.

Brooke's dress was resplendent. It would be hard for her not to look attrac-tive in a pair of worn-out sweats, but in this case she outdid even her reputa-tion, donning a long train and wearing a stunning tiara made from hand-cut Austrian crystal. Her dress was made of Empress satin and embroidered with Schiffli lace.

The Reverend Max Helton from Motor Racing Outreach performed the ceremony, and Brooke softly cried her way through it. Jeff tried to encourage her to master her tears by whispering, "Just don't look at your mother!"

The wedding reception was held at the Founders' Hall, and guests were dazzled by a seven-foot-high wedding cake. The traditional first dance was to "I Swear," and Brooke and Jeff clung tightly together on the dance floor. One photo shows them with their eyes closed, noses barely touching, lost in the joyous moment.

They were sent on their way with showers of rose petals (instead of birdseed) and carted off in a horse-drawn carriage.

Jeff and Brooke honeymooned on St. Martin, in the Caribbean, then flew to New York for the annual NASCAR awards banquet in early December. Before the banquet, held at the Waldorf-Astoria Hotel, Brooke urged Jeff to prepare for his speech. As the eighth-place finisher for the year, he'd be expected to say a few words. But Jeff had no interest in writing out a speech; he didn't even scribble a few notes. Instead, he opted to talk from the heart and include a touching verbal tribute to Brooke.

As the media swarmed the new couple that night, the groom continued to put the focus on his new bride. "It was really fun for me because now I'm married, I get to say 'wife,'" he said. "For so long, it's like 'girlfriend,' 'fiancée.' And I was finally able to say, 'My beautiful wife.' So that was a perfect place to do it at, really the first time."

Brooke provided a missing piece in Jeff's life—a friend and contemporary who could fit into his chaotic schedule. Mark Stewart, an early biographer of Jeff, quotes him as saying, "It's hard for me to have a lot of friends. I work on the weekends and most other people my age work during the week. When they're hanging out, I'm working. When I'm hanging out, they're working. My closest friend is Brooke, because she's basically the same age I am, and we like the same things, and we do everything together."

Brooke's feelings for Jeff are equally evident. "He's one of these people who can make you sick because whatever he tries he's good at," she teased affectionately.

But Gordon insists that much of his success is due to Brooke's inspiration. "My luck never was the same until I could tell everybody about our relationship," he told Dick Brinster. "Now, I'm very happy away from the racetrack. It helps me stay focused. . . . Keep Brooke happy, because she makes me happy. When she makes me happy, I drive better."

Looking Ahead

Nineteen ninety-four had proved to be a breakthrough year for Jeff Gordon. On a personal level, it couldn't have been any better. On a professional level, Jeff was turning heads. An eighth-place points finish for a sophomore driver is outstanding. Not to mention the two wins and the dozen additional top-ten finishes.

Hendrick, at least, was confident. "The sky's the limit," he predicted. "The first time I saw him race . . . I knew he was something special."

At the same time, other Winston Cup drivers seemed to be getting jealous of the fast-rising youngster. Dale Jarrett spoke for many when he quipped, "It should be illegal to be that young, that good-looking, and that talented."

Had Jarrett known what was in store professionally for Jeff in 1995, he might have called his congressperson and tried to pass a law; Gordon was just getting warmed up.

chapter 13

Chasing the Championship: 1995

"When Gordon ran what he did, Curtis Turner, Fireball Roberts, Joe Weatherly, all them guys up in heaven said, 'I'm glad I ain't running Darlington this weekend.'"

—Veteran driver Darrell Waltrip, 1995

A pit stop requires an enormous amount of furious cooperation. The person working on the rear tire of the driver's side can't be worried that the individual standing over him is busy dumping one of two eleven-gallon containers of gasoline into the car, just inches above his head. Like an ant colony, every worker has to do his job—fast—and then get out of the way.

The modern world of NASCAR has reduced the time in which all that needs to be done to an almost ridiculous seventeen seconds. In less time than it takes an average person to walk out to the mailbox, a good team will change four tires, fully gas a car, take care of the driver, clean out the grilles, wash the window, and sometimes make minor adjustments to the vehicle.

To give you an idea of just how good modern crews have become, consider this: In the 1950s, pit stops could routinely last up to *several minutes*. Great strides were made in the 1960s, and the once seemingly impossible sixty-second barrier for a full-service pit stop was breached. In the early 1970s, pit stops dropped down to between forty and fifty seconds. Now, the Rainbow Warriors aim to get Jeff Gordon out in about seventeen to eighteen seconds.

A lot can go wrong when you're moving that fast, and Gordon's first race in February 1995 made that crystal clear.

Jeff had been leading the Daytona 500 for over fifty laps when he came in for a routine pit. Number 24 was jacked, gassed, cleaned, and Jeff was "serviced" all in good time.

But one of the crew missed a lug nut on the front wheel. That set in motion a frustrating string of events. The tire changer was surprised when he yanked on the wheel and it wouldn't come off. He yanked harder, but the lug nut kept the tire in place. He then spotted the troublesome lug nut in front of him and looked down to find the power wrench so that he could take it off.

Communication fell apart. The jack man assumed the fireman had backed away because his job was finished. He dropped the car and that was all the notice Jeff needed.

"As soon as I felt the tire go down, I popped the clutch and started out," Jeff explained to the media after the race.

The tire came off and the front end sustained significant body damage. The race wasn't over, but first place was certainly out of reach. Jeff managed to salvage a twenty-second-place finish.

"We just gave the race away," Ray Evernham, Jeff's crew chief, lamented afterward. "It's just a shame."

It was a frustrating start for the year, but not so frustrating that others couldn't see the potential. Corporate behemoth Kellogg's opted to sign up as an official sponsor of Jeff Gordon's Fan Club. Within months, boys and girls across the country were staring at Jeff's face as they sat in front of boxes of Frosted Mini-Wheats (over two million were distributed with Jeff's photo). Not so surprisingly, his Fan Club base blossomed to over six thousand members.

They were coming aboard with perfect timing. Gordon was getting ready to take them for the ride of their lives.

Consistency

Now that Jeff had placed fourteenth (1993) and eighth (1994) at the end-of-year points standings, he could be considered a legitimate contender for a championship, but Ray Evernham told reporters he was sticking to his "five-year plan," which would result in Jeff being crowned for the first time in 1997. "People tell me it won't take that long, but you can look at what happened in the Daytona 500 in the pits and see that it will," Evernham said. "You've got to go through a lot of heartbreaks before you can win the title.

"I'm watching Richard Childress, and I see what his formula is. You've got to keep the same people together to win a championship. It just takes dedication and hard work."

The key to a championship is consistency. But Jeff had never placed well in Bristol, Tennessee. To win the end-of-year points race, Jeff and his crew would have to master all tracks, including short ones.

This is due to the points system, which was developed in 1975 by Bob Latford. Since NASCAR is run on many different tracks, it is designed to reward drivers who do well in many different venues—not just superspeedways, but road tracks, short tracks, et cetera. Thus it gives preference to consistency over occasional brilliance.

First place in a Winston Cup race is awarded 175 points, followed by 170 points for second, and 165 for third, reducing the points by 5 until sixth place, where the reduction is by 4: 151 points, 147 points, et cetera. Cars finishing eleventh all the way to last (usually forty-third) place receive points in smaller increments of 3.

In addition to the driver's finish, a participant can earn 5 bonus points for leading any one lap in a race, as well as 5 bonus points for leading the most laps in a race—meaning the most you can get, taking both bonuses, is 185 points per race.

In the unlikely event of a tie at the end of a season, the standoff is broken by the greatest number of wins, and then the highest number of second-place finishes, third-place finishes, et cetera.

The system does two things: First, it forces a driver to be consistent. You can win fifteen races in a season and still be defeated by someone who won two races if you finish poorly in the bulk of the other races. (The modern-era record is thirteen wins in a single season, shared by Richard Petty and Jeff Gordon.) The system also encourages drivers to show up for every one of the thirty-plus races. With so many points on the line, a driver is not likely to win the championship if he takes several weeks off.

Slightly chagrined about the pit fiasco at Daytona, the Rainbow Warriors and the number 24 car trailer lumbered into Rockingham, North Carolina, on February 26, 1995, for the Goodwrench 500. In NASCAR, it's "another week, another race."

Gordon kept his head and won the pole, then went on to dominate the race, virtually wearing everyone out by leading 329 of the 492 laps. It was a battle of the youngsters, as both twenty-three year-old Gordon and thirty-one-year-old Bobby Labonte (both three-year drivers) battled it out at the finish. Jeff took the checkered flag for his third Winston Cup victory.

A disappointing thirty-sixth-place finish at Richmond (caused by a malfunctioning fuel pump) was followed by a stunner in Atlanta on March 12. Two seconds is a huge lead in NASCAR, but Jeff managed to push number 24 to a *seventeen*-second lead until Bobby Labonte came up for the challenge. Jeff didn't fold, but hung on to take the flag and first place. Gordon delighted his young fans by celebrating the win with a dust-raising 360-degree spin at the start/finish line.

Four races, two wins.

Gaining Respect

Writer Paul Hemphill is surely right when he says every track on the NASCAR circuit has its own personality, and the track in Darlington, North Carolina, is widely known as "the meanest asphalt ever laid by man." Hemphill points out that it was built in 1950 for an earlier generation of race cars, and now that modern cars run nearly twice as fast as those earlier versions, Darlington's foundation and its little peccadilloes—bumps, ripples, narrowness—just aren't predictable enough.

In his book, *Wheels* (1997), Hemphill quotes veteran driver Rusty Wallace describing races at Darlington: "It's like running through a mine field at a hundred and sixty miles an hour." Earnhardt adds, "It has an invisible hand that'll slap you if you're not paying attention." A NASCAR team manager sums it up: "I'm always saying you need a couple of breaks to win a race, but here you need about four." Even its nickname is more reminiscent of a rodeo bull than a stretch of asphalt: "Too Tough to Tame."

When Richard Petty was asked why all the drivers run so close to the wall in turn four he said, "The closer you are to the wall, the less it hurts when you hit it."

In short, Darlington is a track that requires expert driving, a crew team that makes no mistakes, and an innovative style of racing.

With a track this feared, it means something special when a veteran, such as Darrell Waltrip (who ranks third in the overall number of wins in Winston Cup history), watches in awe as Jeff attacks the track that supposedly can't be beaten and wins the pole during qualifying.

Jeff dominated the early half of the Darlington race, but NASCAR is a sport of surprises, and Jeff found his when another driver spun out in front of the number 24 car. Well, Gordon was blocked by other cars from going either left or right, so he had to go into Randy LaJoie, sustaining enough damage to his own car to knock him out of the race.

Jeff felt his loss deeply. Even after a qualifying run that made hardened veterans like Waltrip stand up and take notice, his crash and thirty-second-place finish grated on him.

"I guess the ego around the garage area is that you're not a real race-car driver until you've won at Darlington," Brinster quotes Jeff as saying. "I believe that as much as anybody else."

To make matters worse, the schedule called for the next race to be held at Bristol (Tennessee), the track where Jeff had never completed a race, much less placed. The foreboding high-banked half-mile oval had proven too tough to master in the past.

But Gordon would be ready for it this time.

Breakthrough at Bristol

For most of the race, the 1995 Food City 500 was a classic battle between Mark Martin and Jeff Gordon. Though Jeff started on the outside pole, he never saw the lead until the forty-first lap. Early on, it was a clean race, with no cautions in the first hundred laps. After that, Dale Earnhardt's furious charge from twenty-fifth to third place was cut short when a collision with Jeff Burton sent number 3 sprawling into the wall.

Jeff had his hands full with a tight car, but the more he ran it, the looser it got. (When a car's steering is called "loose," it means that the car has a tendency to slip or slide too far out when the driver turns a corner. A "tight" car is the opposite—it tends to be unresponsive to a driver's attempt to turn.) Even so, Jeff thought there was no way he could catch Mark Martin. When he finally reached and then passed the leader, Jeff was as surprised as anyone. "All of a sudden Mark started coming back to me, and I couldn't believe it," the racer told Deb Williams, writing for *Winston Cup Scene* (April 6, 1995). "I thought he was letting up just to cool his tires or something. We got up to him and then we went by him, and I couldn't believe it."

Not one to waste a good opportunity, Jeff got busy. "I tried to get through lapped traffic and put as many cars between me and him as I could."

He practically coasted to a 5.74-second victory over Rusty Wallace.

The win catapulted Jeff into fourth place in the Winston Cup standings, and crowned him as the only driver at this point in the 1995 season who had led every race.

The media machine started heating up to the new sensation and veteran Dale Earnhardt started publicly referring to Gordon as "Wonder Boy." Lest anyone think that was a compliment, Earnhardt stressed "Boy" more than "Wonder."

Independence Day

Not that long before the country celebrated its declaration of freedom on July 4, 1995, Jeff had a similar declaration of his own. A surprising announcement from the Gordon team acknowledged that Jeff had hired someone other than his parents to begin managing his business.

"I wanted to start making some decisions for myself, to be able to grow from it. A lot like Brooke Shields," he explained to *Details* magazine in

1997. It was a quiet announcement, but a major one in Jeff's maturity—and one that reflected not only his escalating presence, but also, ironically enough, the strong character of John and Carol Bickford.

"Jeff was married, had his own family, and he wanted to branch off like so many kids do when they start their own families," Bickford told me. "Do his own thing, and that's what he did."

The press was eager to create a family feud here, but Bickford didn't give them any ammunition. In fact, his response to me was brilliantly diplomatic. "A forty-year-old with lots of experience will do something one way, and a kid who is twenty-three will do things differently. I think he conducted himself better than most twenty-three-year-olds would conduct themselves. I think he did a great job with something that was probably very difficult for him."

Carol's take is that starting his own management company was a necessary career step for Jeff. "You raise your children to be responsible, self-supporting adults. That's what life is all about. You don't raise them to cling to [their parents]. You bring your children up to let them go."

Ready to Roll

On his own and ready to roll for the rest of the 1995 season, Jeff came back and won a nonpoints race at Charlotte. While the victory helped fatten his wallet it did nothing to bring him any closer to the Intimidator in the points race. Earnhardt was in good shape and highly motivated to break the record of seven Winston Cup championships, which he shared with Richard Petty.

The drivers stayed in Charlotte for the next race, but the track wasn't nearly so kind to number 24, with Jeff slipping into a thirty-third-place finish. The points race was heating up, but Jeff was insistent that he wasn't looking toward the championship—yet. "We don't think about championship; we don't talk about championship," biographer Dick Brinster quotes Jeff as saying midway through the season. "We just get ready for the next race."

Gordon was able to salvage a sixth-place finish at Dover (Delaware) on June 4, and then seemed poised to win the UAW-GM Teamwork 500 at the Pocono track in Pennsylvania the following week. Jeff was fighting for the lead with Dale Jarrett as he rolled into the pits. But, instead of a first-place finish, Jeff rambled home sixteenth, costing him sixty precious Winston Cup points.

Jeff soon put the past behind him and got back on the winning track at the Pepsi 400 on July 1. It was a hard-fought race in which Jeff barely held off rivals Earnhardt and Sterling Marlin. A quick pit kept Jeff out front. "We had a great pit stop," he told reporters. "We lost this thing in the pits in February, but they won this one for us in the pits."

By now, journalists took notice that a major new driver had come on to the Winston Cup scene. Dick Brinster wrote, "Gordon [already has] victories at Indianapolis, Charlotte, and Daytona, the three great American racetracks. If he . . . announced his retirement [today], his career would already [be] a success."

Gordon claimed the $50,000 Gatorade bonus for leading the points race midway through the 1995 season. Now he was attracting the attention of major media sources that don't exclusively cover NASCAR, such as *Sports Illustrated.* These articles inevitably pointed out that Jeff was poised to become the youngest driver in the modern NASCAR era to win a championship—and thus was in excellent shape to become the best driver of all time—but Jeff showed how focused he was on this season: "I don't sit and think, man, can I win seven championships, or ten championships?" Jeff told *Sports Illustrated*'s Ed Hinton (April 24, 1995). "I'm just going for that first one."

Ray Evernham kept insisting that Jeff's and the Rainbow Warriors' relative inexperience weren't up to the strain of a thirty-one-race championship. But, he would allow, "we are ahead of where we thought we'd be."

At twenty-three and in just his third full season of Winston Cup competition, Jeff still seemed much too inexperienced to win the entire championship, but to be so far up front—in fact, at the very top—after half a season of racing, was rather impressive. In fact the press picked up Earnhardt's moniker, and put the emphasis back on "Wonder Boy."

As the season wore on, Dale Earnhardt became less eager to talk about "the Kid." When Joseph Siano (*New York Times*) approached Dale once again and said he wanted to ask him something about Jeff, Earnhardt melo-dramatically threw up his hands and said, "Go somewhere else!"

The 1995 season looked golden, but Jeff was about to enter the race that, according to him, constituted the worst moment in his racing career to date.

The Wreck

Wrecks typify what makes NASCAR competition so intense. If Shaquille O'Neal gets a little too aggressive on the basketball court, the most that can happen is a poked eye or a harmless slap, punishable by a couple of foul shots.

In NASCAR, one "foul" can create hundreds of thousands of dollars of damage and cripple (or even kill) a competitor. It takes a strong mind to keep going under these grueling conditions.

During the Die-Hard 500 at Talladega (Alabama) on July 23, 1995, Jeff kept looking for a way to squeeze by Kenny Schrader. Jeff finally saw—or at least thought he saw—enough space to slip past Schrader. The pass looked complete and perfect until Jeff looked back and watched his friend literally flipping through the air.

Jeff got sick to his stomach.

Somewhere, the number 24 car must have touched Schrader's car, who then got tangled up with Ricky Craven's vehicle. It created an ugly, ugly wreck, and seriously rattled Jeff's nerves. Ray Evernham kept assuring Jeff over the headphone that both Schrader and Craven were okay, and that Jeff had to forget about the wreck and keep driving.

After the tough event, Schrader was a good sport. Though he looked ugly (one eye was swollen shut), he assured Jeff that he had no hard feelings.

"It upset me a lot," Gordon told Siano, "because here I caused him to have a bad accident, along with a lot of other guys. And that could have been something that tore the whole team apart."

A rattled Jeff finished eighth in that race and then traveled to Indianapolis for a race on August 5 (he had turned twenty-four the day before), where he just narrowly avoided another wreck—this one in the qual-ifying round. One of the challenges of NASCAR is that even when you are running strong, you are never more than a tenth of a second away from running into an outside wall.

That's what happened as Jeff charged into the final turn during qualifying. His splits (interval times taken during the two qualifying laps) were the best of the day and the pole looked like a lock until Jeff's car slid out toward the wall. That slide could have crippled Jeff's car, but Gordon handled it expertly, easing up on the gas and keeping the car away from the wall while still maintaining enough speed to win the pole.

It was an impressive show, to say the least, but the next day there were five drivers between Jeff and the eventual winner, Dale Earnhardt, when the checkered flag fell.

Team 24 garnered two consecutive third-place finishes at Watkins Glen (New York) and Brooklyn (Michigan), then took sixth at the summer Bristol race—a fine stretch of consistent driving.

Doing the Dew

Labor Day weekend is always a sell-out at Darlington, and while the fans were on holiday, Jeff had to work hard at the Mountain Dew Southern 500 in Darlington on September 3.

Jeff was almost taken out early on, surviving a wild spin that he would later credit with actually giving him the victory. The dizzying movement occurred on lap 136 between turns one and two. His car had been running loose all day and suddenly skated out completely. Jeff bumped but didn't crash the wall, preserving a car capable of doing well.

"In a strange way, that spin might have won us the race," Gordon said afterward. "We really didn't have the best car here. We had about a third-place car. . . .

"After the spin, we were on the tail end of the lead lap. We had nothing to lose. We pitted for two fresh tires and then pitted for two more. We threw everything at the car, because that is what it needed.

"The spin put us out-of- sync as far as pit stops were concerned, but we were able to make all the changes we needed."

Ray Evernham agreed with Jeff's analysis. "We wouldn't have won without [the spin]," he admitted.

Jeff's win put him 176 points ahead of Sterling Martin and 294 ahead of Dale Earnhardt with eight races to go in the season. Now that a championship looked realistic, Evernham was ready to scrap his five-year plan and look honestly at taking the championship this year.

"[We're] in a battle for the championship," he said. "We didn't want to be in that frame of mind, but if we weren't in that frame of mind now, we'd be stupid."

But he was adamant that they weren't about to start "stroking" (playing it safe to preserve position instead of going for a win or a top finish).

Six days later, Jeff clocked a sixth-place finish at Richmond, then rolled into Dover Downs like nobody else had a right to be there. After a great second-place qualifying run, Jeff led four-fifths of the 500 laps. It was a commanding performance and showed the Kid was serious about laying claim to his first Winston Cup championship.

Gordon made a respectable showing—seventh place—at Martinsville, followed by a tough third-place run in North Wilkesboro (North Carolina). With just four races to go, he had built a commanding 300-plus points cushion against second-place Dale Earnhardt.

And then things started to fall apart professionally for Gordon.

The Slide

At Charlotte, it was one of those things "that just does not happen," as Jeff put it. A broken ring gear in the back of the car took Gordon out of contention for the win and dropped him into thirtieth place. That opened a window in the points, which Earnhardt exploited.

The October 22 race in Rockingham wasn't much kinder. Jeff finished twentieth, while Earnhardt raced to a seventh-place finish.

The number 24 car's lead was eroding.

The Slick Fifty 500 in Phoenix—the penultimate race of the season—brought back a measure of sanity, and if not security, at least confidence for

Gordon. Once again, Earnhardt finished higher than Jeff—third to the Kid's fifth—but he gained just ten points in the process. That left Jeff with a sufficient enough lead that all he had to do was show up for the next race; a forty-first-place finish out of a field of forty-three would net him the championship.

At Atlanta on November 12, Earnhardt, knowing that the Kid pretty much had the championship locked up, raced aggressively. The Intimidator dominated and then won the last race of the season. And Jeff—well, Jeff rolled to his first championship with a thirty-second-place finish (fourteen laps down at the end). His once comfortable 305-point lead was sliced to a razor-thin 34-point lead, but in a sport where two seconds can mean the difference between first and tenth, 34 points were enough to cement Jeff's victory.

Carol Bickford told me she was actually more overwhelmed by her son's first race victory at Charlotte and his win at the inaugural Brickyard race than by his first championship. "It's huge, but I don't think the championship was as exciting for me as seeing Jeff win his first race."

At forty-three years of age, Earnhardt couldn't get over the fact that he had been beaten by a twenty-four-year-old "kid." "He'll be up there drinking that milk at the front table," Earnhardt quipped.

Crowning the Kid

By "front table," Earnhardt was referring to the head table at the annual (first weekend in December) end-of-season awards banquet. It's held in the grand ballroom of the Waldorf-Astoria in New York City, and may be the hardest ticket to get of any sport's celebration in America. The top-ten drivers get to sit on the stage, but there isn't even enough room for all crew members to actually attend the evening's gala. If you don't know somebody (or practically "own" somebody through sponsorship), don't even bother trying to get in.

In his 1998 book entitled *Wide Open,* Shaun Assael calls the banquet "a dizzying two-day celebration of money and power." Jeff's team owner, Rick Hendrick, chartered a 737 and flew 160 people to New York in celebration of his first championship. And once there, Hendrick paid special tribute to his star driver. "That little gentleman right there," he said, pointing to Jeff, "this year he's been called 'Kid' and 'Flash Gordon,' a little bit of this and a little bit of that, but tonight I want to thank 'the Champ' for giving me my first championship."

Jeff seemed overwhelmed after he was handed the championship check for $1,829,883. "That's a lot of money. I mean a lot of money," he said. "I'm not kidding, that's a lot of money." The crowd started laughing, and Jeff played with them by referring to his older tormentor.

"Dale, you'd say that was a lot of money, too."

A little later, Gordon got everybody's attention and said, "I would like to recognize a man who never let up on his efforts to win his eighth championship. Dale Earnhardt is a true competitor and a great champion, and at this time I would like to offer a toast to 'the Man.'"

Jeff then lifted a carton of milk that had been brought onstage in a champagne bucket and poured himself a nice cold glass.

The crowd erupted into laughter and cheers.

Gordon also paid tribute to his crew chief, Ray Evernham. "How we met wasn't by luck," he said, looking at Ray. "It was truly by God's blessing and fate, but we didn't know it until now. I just really want to thank you for your time and dedication."

When Jeff looked at his mom and dad, and his wife Brooke, he was overcome with emotion. "I'm so glad to see you guys here tonight," he said, pointing to Carol and John. "There are the ones who got it all started a long, long time ago. Who would have known? They did, and I love them."

The three-hour ceremony was televised live on ESPN on December 1, 1995.

During his week in New York, Jeff appeared on David Letterman's late-night TV talk show and on *Good Morning America*. His comments were pure American: "Winning the title is just too good to be true," he said. "There just aren't words to describe how I feel. It's been a spectacular year—better than we ever thought it could be."

It was, he said, the "funnest week of his life."

At twenty-four years of age, Jeff had become the second-youngest driver ever to win a Winston Cup championship. Bill Rexford had won it at the age of twenty-three in 1950, but comparing NASCAR in 1950 to NASCAR in 1995 is a little like comparing slide rules to calculators.

A more modern comparison makes Jeff's accomplishment even more impressive. Earnhardt was twenty-nine when he won his first title. The King, Richard Petty, was twenty-seven when he did the same.

In addition to being crowned Winston Cup champion, Jeff was also named Driver of the Year by a panel of twelve motorsports journalists. The panel can select drivers from all forms of racing—Indy cars, drag racing, et cetera—so winning the Winston Cup by no means automatically crowns a participant Driver of the Year.

It was a profitable year for Gordon as well as a historic one. With post-season bonuses, Jeff ended the year $4,347,343 richer (not including endorsement income). He had won $2,430,460 on the track.

As the Winston Cup champion, Jeff's place in history was already secure, and Earnhardt grudgingly admitted that in 1995, at least, the Kid was "bulletproof." But Earnhardt still had his doubts about the future. Racing journalist Dick Brinster caught him saying, "Winning one championship doesn't make him the greatest driver in the world. He's a good driver, but he's got a long way to go to win 200-plus races and seven or eight championships."

Maybe so, but garnering a championship so young certainly put Jeff Gordon in position to challenge history's best.

chapter 14

Lifestyle of a Champion

"Jeff and Brooke are doing things smart."
—Carol Bickford, 1998

"I get carsick if I'm not driving. . . . I'm not very good in traffic. If it's bumper-to-bumper, I get a little frustrated."
—Jeff Gordon, 1997

What's it like to be Jeff Gordon? For starters, it's busier than most people could possibly imagine. Employees who complain about forty-hour work-weeks would have difficulty adapting to a schedule that requires ninety hours a week or more.

"If you look at the calendar of a Winston Cup champion," John Bickford explained to me, "you'll find out that there's no scheduling in there for family members and things like that. It's consumed by the business of racing. There is no time. You have minutes, but no time. That's part of the life of racing."

In 1997, to take advantage of two newly built tracks (one in Fontana, California, and the other in Fort Worth, Texas), NASCAR bumped the number of races up from thirty-one to thirty-two. The year 1998 saw no fewer than thirty-three races (with another two exhibition races held in Japan after the regular season ended) and the 1999 schedule called for thirty-four races. Older drivers like Rusty Wallace complained that NASCAR, starting out with quality, was descending into quantity, and even the younger Jeff remarked in 1996 to a *New York Times* reporter, "I'm young and I've got energy and I do a lot of things for my sponsors right now, but I don't know if I can go on that schedule forever."

The reason for the additional new races is quite simple: money. Fontana seats 80,000 people and is being enlarged to accommodate almost forty thousand more. The new Texas Motor Speedway can welcome 151,000 fans on a single afternoon. Ticket sales, not to mention two additional days of television revenue, bring in millions of dollars. The exhibition races in Japan constitute an effort to make NASCAR more of an international sport. This search for an ever-widening base, not to mention a larger source of revenue, is stretching the season to almost absurd lengths—nearly ten months a year.

Even apart from the demands of actual competition, it's difficult for fans to understand how overwhelming it is just managing the responsibilities of a successful NASCAR career.

"You've got to learn how to say no," Jeff explained once. "You've got to learn how to make sure you're fulfilling your commitments, but most of all you've got to fulfill your commitment to the race team and to what really is making this all go around."

Referring to all the professional expectations of NASCAR competition, Geoff Bodine, a fellow driver, told Richard Huff (author of *The Insider's Guide to Stock-car Racing*), "What life? Once you're in Daytona, your life is over. It's owned by the racing gods."

Travel alone is a killer. Jeff has estimated that he spends well over four hundred hours a year on airplanes—that's three times longer than he spends actually racing. That's why it's not so much a luxury as a necessity for Jeff to travel to races in his own Lear jet or motor home.

A Week in the Life

In his photo-essay, Jeff provides readers with a brief glimpse into his life: "Monday is [my and Brooke's] day to recuperate, kind of unwind, relax at home, and get things done around the house. We unpack, sort through the mail, get caught up with phone calls, and sometimes go out to eat lunch. . . ."

Tuesday usually finds Jeff responding to requests from the media or making an appearance for a sponsor or charity. Wednesday, it's usually back to work, doing stuff in his office (when he lived in Charlotte, he'd sometimes stop in at Hendrick Motorsports). Thursdays are typically a travel day. Jeff goes to the city where the race is being held that week and then often does a local appearance.

Friday, of course, usually means practice runs and qualifying. Saturday is spent getting prepped for the race, and Sunday is consumed with being the fastest man on four wheels.

For post-race nourishment, Gordon prefers "filling" foods. "After a race, I'm usually starving, . . ." he explains. "I want the most filling thing I can find."

Usually, the saltier the food, the better. When you've been eating exhaust for three or four hours, your taste buds need to be shocked awake, so Jeff has been known to down an entire jar of olives or pickles after a long contest. If it's not salty, he likes spicy (pizza is another post-race favorite), though he goes light on junk foods at other times.

While he's eating, Jeff often watches the cable show *RPM 2Night* (which Jeff has appeared on frequently). But if the race that day is one Jeff would rather forget about, he and Brooke might take in a movie.

What about the few off-moments? From the time he was in kindergarten, Jeff has been an avid fan of video games—something he still enjoys.

In season or out, Jeff likes to sleep in. "I'm not afraid to say it," he admits. "I'm not a morning person. That's just not who I am. If it's before nine A.M. I have a hard time getting up. . . . That's why I like night races. I can sleep in until noon and get to the racetrack by two and be ready to race. I'm definitely not an early riser."

The Price of Fame

Whether Jeff is now NASCAR's most famous driver is questionable; whether he and Brooke are NASCAR's most famous couple probably is not.

To *Carolina Bride* magazine, Jeff admitted, "It has been great for me to have some of the spotlight on Brooke and off me. Since we've been together, she has become sort of a landmark. Fans recognize her before they do me. They've learned to look for her because wherever she is, they know I'll be there soon."

When the two are together, Brooke rarely drives. "Jeff's not a good passenger," Brooke mentioned to *Details* magazine in 1997. "He critiques everything: 'Get in this lane, it's going faster.'"

In his defense, Gordon says, "I get carsick if I'm not driving. I don't like putting my life in other people's hands."

Though the money, the beautiful wife, the fame, seeing his face on television and billboards, on toothpaste containers, soda machines, cereal boxes, and a plethora of authorized toys must be intoxicating, fame comes at a price.

While Jeff and Brooke once resided in a North Carolina lakefront home, some unruly fans have taken that option away. Rusty Wallace, who lives less than a mile down the shore from where Jeff used to live in Harrisburg, North Carolina, told *Sports Illustrated* writer Ed Hinton, "It's terrible when you've got to sit in your house with the blinds drawn. People with binoculars will sit in boats at my seawall, and they'll stare and stare. Boatloads of them will yell, 'Hey, Rusty! H-e-e-y Rusty! . . . Then they go down to Gordon's house. They're driving Jeff ape. That's the reason he's moving to Boca Raton [Florida]."

On one Memorial Day, Wallace counted seventy boats milling around in front of his house. A particularly bold and unruly fan actually jumped on to his property and went up to the windows of Wallace's home, trying to peer in.

It's unnerving. For example, Brooke once heard a noise outside their North Carolina home and looked out to investigate. A man sitting on the windowsill was videotaping their cat.

But celebrity does have its benefits. In March 1996, Jeff and Brooke were invited to several Academy Awards parties in Los Angeles. For once, Jeff was the fan and not the hunted. In fact, many of the movie and television stars didn't even know who he was. However, Jeff and his wife had the chance to mingle with the likes of Cindy Crawford, Tom Cruise, Steve Martin, Woody Harrelson, and Leonardo DiCaprio. The experience of being a relative "unknown" among other megasuperstars gave Jeff a new understanding of his own status as a celebrity and how, in turn, his fans feel about him.

As a sports celebrity, even ordinary situations take on a competitive flavor for Jeff. On one occasion, he was running late for a flight and a cop stopped him for speeding. "I'm Jeff Gordon," he said. "Do you follow racing?"

The cop didn't miss a beat. He tore off a piece of paper and said, "Yeah, here's your ticket. I'm a Dale Earnhardt fan."

Brooke Gordon goes to all the races. "When he gets in a race car, I want to be with him," she explained to *People* magazine in 1997. These days, they're likely to get there in their Lear jet 35A. They also own a custom-fitted, 45-foot motor coach, a 29-foot speedboat, and a cherry-red Jaguar XK8 (a Christmas gift to Brooke from Jeff).

The demands of fame and its financial rewards makes friendship problematic. "Not too many people our age are in our tax bracket," Gordon admitted to David Handelman of *Details.* "That becomes an issue—from their side, usually. Jealousy, things like that."

Jeff handles the lure of money in two ways: by saying no to opportunities that go against his principles and by giving a good bit of it away.

For example, this celebrity has been known to turn down some extremely lucrative opportunities (some estimates put the offers at half a million dollars or more each), including endorsement contracts from several breweries. "I'm image-conscious," Jeff explained, "especially since I got married, and doing beer commercials, that's just not me. I know people have criticized me as being phony, but that's not true. I have a happy life, a wonderful wife, and I try not to do things that go counter to that atmosphere."

And when he's not earning money on the track or through endorsement deals, he is helping to raise it for good causes.

In one recent year, Jeff entertained thirty-five children from the Toledo Children's Hospital; visited a young girl in desperate medical straits (her spine curvature was so severe that it was causing her lungs to collapse); consoled a boy whose father was killed at a grandstand accident in Michigan; and cooperated for several visits with the Make-A-Wish Foundation.

Another charity Gordon has pledged to support is the development of Speediatrics, a racing-themed pediatric unit at the Halifax Medical Center, just one mile from the Daytona International Speedway in Florida.

"I wish I had more time to do things like that," Jeff told the *Los Angeles Times*. "It really gives me a good feeling."

Because of Ray-J's (Evernham's son) and team owner Rick Hendrick's own experiences with cancer, Jeff has joined his teammates in fighting leukemia and supporting bone-marrow donations. In one year, Jeff, Terry Labonte, and Ricky Craven raised $600,000—which is almost as much as the National Marrow Donor Program raised. They also helped recruit seventeen thousand new bone-marrow donors.

Explaining his volunteer work to help fight leukemia, Jeff says, "I know it's hard to believe, but racing is not the first thing on my priority list. My life away from racing is certainly more important. The more successful I am, the more I want to do."

Gordon also gives his time to Christian causes, such as Promise Keepers and MRO (Motor Racing Outreach). "I'll go and speak out at churches and different events to kind of give my testimony on the Lord and show my faith," he explains on his Web page.

Jeff's principled stands can be surprising. He approached R. J. Reynolds and said he wanted to do a commercial warning kids not to smoke. In essence, he approached the Winston Cup sponsor and said, "I'd like you to pay for me to tell young kids not to buy your products." (Gordon wasn't paid for his time, but Reynolds paid for the production expenses.) The anti-tobacco climate was reaching a fevered pitch, and RJR readily agreed.

There's no question: Gordon makes a lot of money and is quickly becoming a household name. "Money and fame can cause more heartache than happiness if you don't handle them properly," Carol Bickford told me. "If you get all caught up in the fame and fortune and don't take a few steps back to look at what's really important, well, you see rich people commit suicide all the time."

In spite of the difficulties of fame and fortune, Carol sees Jeff and Brooke handling their situation very well.

"Jeff and Brooke are doing things smart," she says.

chapter 15

Defending the Title: January–July 1996

"Winning one championship doesn't make him the greatest driver in the world. He's a good driver, but he's got a long way to go to win 200-plus races and seven or eight championships."

—Dale Earnhardt, 1996

As soon as January 1996 rolled around, the Gordon team must have been thinking, "How do we top last year?" Seven wins, eight poles, winning more money and leading more laps than any other driver, the Winston Cup championship. . . . What can you do for an encore?

Gordon was enthusiastic as he faced the press. "I still can't believe what's happening," he said. "My career started, then skyrocketed, and then *boom!* God was certainly on our side all last year."

A preseason poll of motorsports journalists revealed that while God may have been on Jeff's side, most writers weren't. Only one in ten thought Jeff Gordon would repeat his championship performance in 1996. Maybe the media thought 1995 was just a fluke, or that Jeff was too young to string together back-to-back titles. More likely, they simply thought the competition was too strong. Dale Earnhardt was the clear favorite, with 51 percent picking him to win.

Two other drivers, Terry Labonte and Rusty Wallace, also edged out Gordon in this preseason poll. Though Jeff had dominated the year before, few writers bet on him doing it again.

Earnhardt did not even wait until Daytona to begin his competition. For him, the 1996 season had started back at the December 1995 awards banquet in New York city when he intimated that he might not be so "easy" on Jeff this year.

Gordon wasn't awed. Referring to Earnhardt's bump-and-grind racing tactics, Jeff told the *New York Times,* "I'm the kind of person who won't do that unless it's done to me. And if it happens to me, I can deal with it."

The lack of media confidence in Gordon and his number 24 team caught Evernham off-guard. On Jeff's Web site, Ray confesses, "We were surprised that the media didn't pick us in the top three [for 1996]. That's done nothing but motivate the heck out of us. We had that article framed and hung it up so we could look at it every day. We appreciate Earnhardt being favored to beat us. That did more to fire up my guys than anything I could have done. We're pretty intense right now."

Regardless of what the experts were predicting, Jeff's showing in 1995 earned him the coveted champion's spot in the Daytona garage. This favored location always goes to the previous year's winner—sort of like the CEO having the best parking place in front of an office building. Each team is granted a particular spot on which the cars can be adjusted and fine-tuned, and Jeff thought being in the champion's area was a "thrill."

That thrill, unfortunately, would be short-lived.

Boom!

The 1996 season certainly didn't get off to a propitious start. On February 18, Gordon became Daytona's (and therefore the season's) first casualty. It happened, not surprisingly, on Daytona's "tunnel bump," a well-known track distinction created by the tunnel that leads into the infield. Jeff and Jeremy Mayfield got tangled up as Jeff attempted to squeeze into position, and the bump made any corrective moves practically futile. Jeff's car slammed into the wall.

Hard.

A writer found Gordon, drenched in sweat, looking at the Rainbow Warriors as they worked feverishly to put number 24 back together. "I got to the outside of Mayfield going into turn three," Gordon explained to Paul Hemphill, who was writing his book, *Wheels*. "I was up against the wall as far as I could get to make sure we didn't touch. I had a feeling something was going to happen, and it did."

Two hours later, Ray Evernham was able to ignite the engine and everybody tried not to wince at the blue smoke that poured from the exhaust. Ray called for Gordon, and less than sixty seconds later, the young driver was by his side. Evernham shouted his directions, pointing to the car, telling Jeff what to watch out for and Jeff reentered the race, 105 laps behind.

It was one of those days. When Evernham radioed Jeff to find out how the car was doing, the news wasn't good.

"It's slow; it's pulling," Jeff said.

"Better bring it on in, then," Evernham responded. "We don't want to do any more damage."

As the most prestigious race, with broadcast coverage, Daytona has deeper pockets than most races. Additionally, as the Winston Cup champion, Jeff receives appearance money, so his thirteen laps and forty-second-place finish still earned him over $59,000, but it wasn't the way he wanted to start the year. In fact, it was his worst Winston Cup finish ever.

Maybe that's why in a startlingly short period of time—less than ten minutes—Jeff was out of his uniform and promising reporters that he'd be back for Rockingham. He and Brooke left the track and had to listen on the radio to find out that Jarrett had managed to stave off a very eager, Daytona 500-deprived Dale Earnhardt.

Working for a Win

With such a disappointing finish in the first race of the year, Jeff was hungry for a good showing at Rockingham for the Goodwrench 500. He barely got a nibble, however, as he suffered a blown engine about a third of the way through the event.

Fortieth place. His second-worst Winston Cup showing ever. Jeff completed less than a third of the total laps in the first two races—just 147 of 593.

Maybe the pundits were right. After all, Earnhardt took the race, starting the season with impressive second- and first-place finishes.

It doesn't take much—a five-minute rain delay will suffice—for Winston Cup fans to start gossiping and second-guessing what's happening. And the word around the track was that maybe Ray Evernham had bitten off more than he could chew when he agreed to manage two cars in 1996—Jeff's car, and the Hendrick-team number 25 car, driven by Ricky Craven. (On race day, Ray's focus was entirely on Jeff; Ricky had a crew chief of his own.) Maybe Jeff's cars just weren't prepared well enough.

"We've been humbled," Jeff confessed to reporters before the Pontiac Excitement 400, held on March 3 in Richmond, Virginia. It had been a depressing February, and the third race of the season was getting under way. The conditions were less than ideal—a dreary, dark winter day, with possible snow flurries in the forecast.

Richmond International Raceway is a short track, three-quarters of a mile long, with about as intimate a setting as you can get for NASCAR. It accommodates less than 90,000, and the seats are positioned right up against the track. The larger tracks have infield camping, where fans can buy tickets that allow them to camp out in the infield and watch the race from inside the track. But Richmond's size precludes this.

Terry Labonte won the pole in qualifying, but Jeff started in the number two spot. The drivers were concerned about heating up the tires. (Cold tires have less traction, so a driver will often swerve back and forth to "heat them up.") Meanwhile the fans were trying to stay warm in temperatures that would never climb higher than the forties. Racetrack organizers decreed an unusually long five-lap pacing at the start to warm up the cold tires, but there was nothing they could do about the freezing fans.

Though Jeff had led periodically throughout the day, he entered the pit running fifth; the Rainbow Warriors got him out in first, helped in part by Jeff having the best pit area (located at the very end). Ray adjusted the number 24 car's tire pressure to give Jeff better handling.

Yellow caution flags started popping up like dandelions. Drivers were getting testy; they started taking chances, and a lot of sheet metal was bending as a result. Restarts are always daunting for the leader, but Jeff held up, maintaining his position each time. A final caution came out with just five laps to go. Evernham reached for the words that would get the deed done. With two terrible finishes, Jeff desperately needed a win.

Hemphill caught the action. "Okay, Jeff," Evernham said as the cars slowly circled the track, getting ready for the green flag to drop. "You're the Winston Cup champion. Now sit up straight in your seat, and let's win this thing."

As soon as the green flag dropped, Jeff nailed the restart. It was a perfect piece of driving, and the other drivers swallowed nothing but exhaust. Nobody was going to catch him now.

The Rainbow Warriors knew they had it won. Jeff still had two laps to go when Evernham got on the radio and said, "I can't tell you how proud I am of you today, Jeff."

Over Hill, Over Dale . . .

The next week in Atlanta was another strong showing for Jeff. He came back from a twenty-first-place qualifying to claim third place, but Earnhardt maintained his dominance in the points standing by winning the race. His two firsts and one second showed that Earnhardt was serious about taking home his eighth championship in 1996.

From Atlanta, the haulers moved to Darlington, South Carolina. Twelve cars never made it across the finish line, and of those that did, only seven made it on the lead lap.

Jeff led them all. The specter of two debilitating losses early in the season was finally exorcised by three excellent showings—two wins and one third-place finish. Jeff eked into the top-ten in the standings.

The Rainbow Warriors were back.

Driving Under Terry's Spotlight

One thing you can count on: You'll never see a Super Bowl played in Bristol, Tennessee (population: 23,200). You'll never see a World Series game or an NBA final there, either. This town, tucked away almost all by itself in the northeastern corner of the state, is over a hundred miles from Knoxville. However, twice a year, you can watch the best drivers in the world chase each other for a furious five hundred miles.

The track at Bristol is, well, unique. In his literary purview, Richard Petty (who has won more NASCAR races than any driver in history) said, it "looks like one o' them county-fair deals for motorbikes." It was built well before the modern era of NASCAR. For that matter, it was built a decade before Jeff Gordon was even born.

It's a concrete, half-mile track with the most steeply banked turns on the circuit. Qualifying speeds typically run well over 50 mph slower than at other tracks, and races are almost always run in tight packs.

March 31—race day—bloomed rainy and dark. Rain delays added almost an hour and a half to the actual race time.

Mark Martin exploded off the pole to establish a lead that lasted for the first sixty laps. After lap sixty, Bill Elliott and Mike Skinner traded the lead for about another forty laps, until Gordon got his car up there and stayed in front.

Then the rain returned, and with it, near-chaos. An unusually sudden red flag (which halts a race) had the same effect on the teams as stomping on an anthill has on ants; nobody expected a quick pit, so nobody knew where they were supposed to go. Some cars even pulled into the wrong pits.

In the pandemonium, the Rainbow car somehow came out first, and Jeff held on to his lead until yet another red flag stopped the race for over an hour. Over three hundred of the five hundred scheduled laps had been completed, and the drivers waited to see when the race would be restarted.

Gordon was on live television (ESPN), doing an interview, when Dale Earnhardt broke in and said, "You win. Congratulations. I'm outta here."

Officials, guessing that the weather wouldn't lift anytime in the foreseeable future, had decided to call the race. Since Jeff had been in the lead, he was declared the winner.

After two disastrous starts, he ended up winning three out of the first six races. Most drivers would consider three wins a good season, but Jeff was just warming up.

The next week at North Wilkesboro (North Carolina), Jeff's teammate Terry Labonte tied Richard Petty for the most consecutive starts. All eyes were on the Kellogg's-sponsored car, and Terry put on a good show, dueling with Rusty Wallace for the lead throughout.

Jeff caught a break when John Andretti took out Wallace, allowing the number 24 car to challenge Labonte, but Terry held him off and completed his day perfectly, demonstrating that he can also win. Starting from the seventeenth position, Jeff was happy to take second in the event.

The following week—April 21—attention was once again focused on NASCAR iron man Terry Labonte, who was about to break Richard Petty's record 513 starts. It was a phenomenal, Cal Ripken Jr.-like feat.

Wallace took the checkered flag and Gordon finished third, racking up an impressive sixth consecutive top-three finish.

Trouble in Talladega

Talladega (Alabama) is, along with Daytona, one of the fastest tracks on the circuit. It is home to the fastest NASCAR lap ever recorded, Bill Elliott's 212-mph scorcher. As a fast track, Talladega has been host to many tragedies, including the last fatal Winston Cup accident. In 1993, a seven-car collision claimed the life of Stanley Smith, whose helmet cut into his neck and severed an artery. One of the cars in that crash was driven by Jimmy Horton. Horton actually went flying off the track and would later quip, "I knew I'd been in a bad crash when the first guy to reach my car was holding a can of beer."

It is more than a little ironic that in addition to the spring Winston Select 500, the annual fall Die-Hard 500 is held here.

Die hard, indeed.

Paul Hemphill caught Dale Jarrett voicing most drivers' opinions about Talladega: "It's pretty much hell. Anybody that tells you it's not the most nerve-racking place we race, they haven't been up in that lead pack. . . ."

The track is the fastest, and with the NASCAR-prescribed restrictor plates, the scariest—for the simple reason that nobody can get away. Restrictor plates are attached to a vehicle's carburetor, cutting the airflow to the engine and thereby reducing available horsepower. They were designed to slow the cars down and therefore make racing safer, but some drivers feel they do the opposite, because the plates ensure that, just when you need a quick burst of speed to avoid a disaster, NASCAR is holding you back with the iron-clad anchor of a rule. The combination of traveling nearly 200 mph while racing together means a crash is virtually inevitable.

The day before the Winston Select 500, Talladega hosted the International Race of Champions (IROC), which takes top drivers from four different types of racing (Indy cars, NASCAR, World of Outlaws sprint cars, and road racing), puts them all in the same type of car and tells them to go at it.

The problem is that every car handles differently. Asking an Indy-car driver to race a stock car is like asking John Grisham to write a song or John Lennon to write a thriller novel.

Early on in the race, Earnhardt went low to challenge Sterling Marlin for the lead. Marlin bumped the Intimidator from behind, and Earnhardt spun into the wall.

Boom! Boom! Boom! Boom! Boom!

Five cars bit it off Earnhardt's wreck, and Gordon's was one of them. He walked away, not realizing he was about to experience two wrecks in twenty-four hours.

One day later, Talladega became the scene of Jeff's worst and scariest crash to date. Unfortunately, he sort of set it all in motion.

It all began as he found his car being pushed up against the wall. Trying to right the car, he touched Mark Martin. At 180 mph, a "touch" is like being kissed by Randy Johnson's fastball. Martin went sideways into Ward Burton, and there followed one of those NASCAR moments where time stops and nobody breathes.

Near the front of the crash site, where Jeff's DuPont car was ramming into Earnhardt (with Earnhardt's passenger side mashed into the wall), two of Ricky Craven's tires hung suspended in midair. Craven's grotesquely twisted car was turned around and sent airborne, the front end completely demolished. The carburetor was sheared away, and the engine had actually moved to the left side of the car. When Craven landed, he took several additional cars with him.

When metal hits metal at that speed, you don't hear the hollow thud that follows a city fender-bender. It sounds more like an explosion. Gordon remembers, "I just closed my eyes and kept hearing, *boom*."

When he opened his eyes, it looked like he was in a tornado, with car parts swirling around him.

Finally the slamming stopped, the cars quit sliding, and an eerie silence descended as everybody strained to see what was left of Craven's car. Through the smoke and twisted metal, a less-than-enthusiastic arm waved out of 41's window.

Craven was still alive, thank God.

In the devastation, four cars were severely damaged and five others were knocked out of the race. It was one of the worst wrecks in Talladega history, requiring almost an hour (fifty-two minutes and six seconds, to be exact) to clean up.

Gordon's official finish was thirty-third place, but he was no doubt very grateful that he had walked away from the event.

Up Front

Jeff had to put the wreck behind him. Seven days later in Sonoma Jeff finished in sixth place; this was followed by a fourth-place finish at Charlotte in the Coca-Cola 600.

And then it was back to Dover, Delaware, on June 2 for the Dover 500. For the second week in a row, Jeff won the pole, but in accomplishing that feat, history was actually against him. The Dover 500 was twenty-one years old, and in those twenty-one years, the pole-sitter had never taken the checkered flag.

Not one to let superstition get in his way, Jeff was all over the front, leading 307 of the 500 laps—including the final one.

That fine piece of driving was repeated the next weekend, as Jeff took his third consecutive pole at Long Pond, Pennsylvania, for the UAW-GM Teamwork 500. The 2.5-mile track at Long Pond keeps racers busy with its sharp turns and constant demand for gear shifts.

Dale Earnhardt, now leading the points race, went out after the first hundred laps with a broken engine valve, giving Jeff a chance to pick up

Prom King Jeff Gordon (with Prom Queen Deena Waters) at Tri-West High School in Pittsboro, Indiana, 1989. COURTESY OF SETH POPPEL YEARBOOK ARCHIVES

(top) Jeff poses with some of his trophies, November 1988. COURTESY OF TOM DE VETTE

(bottom) Jeff with his Busch series Baby Ruth car, February 1992. COURTESY OF TOM DE VETTE

Jeff and Brooke at the First Baptist Church in Charlotte, North Carolina on November 26, 1994, where they were married. COURTESY OF JOANNA NISBET, PHIL AULL STUDIOS

(top) Jeff and crew chief, Ray Evernham, November 1994. COURTESY OF TOM DE VETTE

(bottom) Winston Cup champion Jeff, with Brooke on his right and team owner Rick Hendrick on his left, 1995. COURTESY OF TOM DE VETTE

Jeff, the NASCAR Winston Cup Series champion of the year, on promotional tour in New York City, November 1995. COURTESY OF MARTY LEDERHANDLER

(top) Jeff celebrates after his victory in the Brickyard 400 at the Indianapolis Motor Speedway, August 1, 1998. COURTESY OF ALL SPORT

(bottom) Jeff showing off his million-dollar check at the same event. COURTESY OF ALL SPORT

(top) Jeff takes a moment to himself at the Primestar 500 in Hampton, Georgia, on March 3, 1998. COURTESY OF ALL SPORT

(bottom) Jeff and Brooke at the NASCAR Goodwrench 400 in North Carolina, on February 22, 1998. COURTESY OF ALL SPORT

(top) Jeff reacts after winning the Daytona 500, at the Daytona International Speedway in Daytona Beach, Florida on February 14, 1999. COURTESY OF CHRIS O'MEARA

(bottom) Jeff poses with crew chief, Ray Evernham, after a practice lap at Pocono International Raceway in Long Pond, Pennsylvania on July 25, 1998. COURTESY OF RUSS HAMILTON

precious points. Not one to squander a golden opportunity, Jeff took his second checkered flag in as many weeks.

Having garnered two straight wins and three consecutive poles, number 24 was looking formidable. "This really hurts," Earnhardt said to the media after the race. "The Kid's team doesn't seem to miss a beat."

However, the Rainbow Warrior's near-perfect pit performance reputation was a bit tarnished at the Miller Genuine Draft 400 in Brooklyn, Michigan, the following week. After a quick pit, NASCAR officials noticed that the number 24 car was missing a lug nut. They ruled that Jeff had to go back to the pits. That cost Jeff dearly, though he still managed to work his way back to sixth by the time the final flag dropped.

The points race for 1996 was now extremely close. Gordon was in third place, just 12 points behind second-place Terry Labonte and 64 points behind Dale Earnhardt.

Hot July

Jeff took another pole and then placed third in the rain-shortened Pepsi 400 at Daytona, but he rolled to a disappointing thirty-fourth (due to ignition problems) at the Slick Fifty 300 in Loudon, New Hampshire, followed by a seventh-place finish at the Miller Genuine Draft 500 in Pennsylvania on July 21.

All this time, Terry Labonte was earning the moniker "Mr. Consistent" as he drove his way past Earnhardt into the Winston Cup lead.

Gordon came back to Talladega, the scene of his worst accident ever, during a scorching July 28 weekend. He had good reason to break his short losing streak: The Winston Cup bonus, given to the points leader halfway through the season, totaled $160,000. If Jeff could race back into the lead, the check would be his.

Gordon qualified second at Talladega, starting on the outside of pole-sitter Jeremy Mayfield. More to the point, the two drivers he had to beat to win the bonus—Earnhardt and Labonte—were back in the pack, fourth and twenty-ninth respectively.

Rains delayed the race that day until late in the afternoon.

Early in the race, John Andretti sent Jarrett into a spin, which ultimately created a twelve-car pileup and a caution. The three points leaders escaped harm, but the next wreck would be a little more momentous, changing the course of the season for one of them.

As it happened, in a mad race for the lead, number 3, driven by Earnhardt, was suddenly airborne, twice, and several cars collided. A driver can't possibly stop fast enough to avoid an accident when he's traveling 180 mph, so pileups happen pretty fast. No less than three cars caromed into Earnhardt's roof, smashing it in with hideous force.

Coming up from behind, Gordon saw a small opening and took it, just managing to escape the flying metal and spinning cars. Though Earnhardt walked away, a season championship seemed in great jeopardy after doctors diagnosed him with a broken collarbone and fractured sternum. It would take weeks for a normal driver to recuperate from such injuries, and the NASCAR schedule doesn't allow racers weeks of grace time. With just a few exceptions, races are held virtually every seven days.

By the time the track had been cleared, impending darkness forced NASCAR to shorten the race. Officials said they would drop the checkered flag at 129 laps, which meant that it would all come down to a five-lap free-for-all after the last caution.

Jarrett took the lead, but Gordon used Jeff Burton's air to rocket past Jarrett in an exciting near-photo finish, with just hundredths of a second separating them.

That 0.14 second propelled Gordon into the Winston Cup lead and made him hundreds of thousands of dollars richer; just as significant, it didn't look like Dale Earnhardt would be back anytime soon. Hendrick Motorsports held the top two spots, with Terry and Jeff chasing each other.

Jeff was pumped up—and sounding young—when he told reporters, "This is a really, really exciting win for us. To take the points lead, that's just unbelievable."

His dominance of the sport was becoming more and more apparent.

chapter 16

The Chase Is on: August—December 1996

"I hope they boo me like that someday."

—Jeff Gordon, 1984

Jeff Gordon won his fifth pole of the season for the next week's race, the August 3 Brickyard 400, but Dale Earnhardt stole the headlines.

Almost unbelievably, Dale Earnhardt refused to kiss his season goodbye. Heads shook and mouths dropped open when word got out that the Intimidator would be back at work on Tuesday. Earnhardt calmly explained that he'd wait until the season was over before he had the necessary surgery to repair his injuries from the previous Sunday's race at Talladega.

Fans were aghast. How in the world was this going to work? How do you drive a car with a broken collarbone and a fractured sternum?

You get creative.

Dale's crew built a special harness that would allow him to start the Brickyard 400. Once the pain became too great or Earnhardt became too tired, a substitute driver, Mike Skinner, would take over. According to NASCAR rules, whoever starts the race gets the points.

Though Gordon started out on the pole, almost immediately the race was halted—mercifully, for Earnhardt. An early caution just six laps into the race gave the Intimidator a chance to bail early.

Jeff's vehicle wasn't handling very well to begin with, so he let a few cars go by. He was looking for a caution so that the Rainbow Warriors could make the necessary adjustments to give him a car that could handle the grueling strain of driving up front. But then his car suddenly lurched toward the wall. He had cut a tire and lost all control. The damage was considerable, and Jeff was out of the race with a thirty-seventh-place finish.

Skinner brought Earnhardt's famous black car home in fifteenth place, so Earnhardt actually gained ground on the Kid while sitting in an RV with his wife watching the race on television!

Dale shocked the NASCAR world the next week by winning the pole on one of the most physically demanding courses on the circuit, the road course at Watkins Glen, New York. Watkins Glen is located just south of Seneca Lake on the western side of the state, about seventy miles southeast of Rochester.

Nobody expected that Earnhardt's beat-up body could endure the grueling movement throughout the day, but Dale's sixth-place finish (to Jeff's fourth) was about as close to legendary as you can get while you're still alive. Though the Kid was picking up most of the wins, Earnhardt was showing that NASCAR's "old stock" still had a lot of miles left in them.

Jeff tagged on a fifth-place finish the next week in Brooklyn (Michigan), then said good-bye to August with a second-place showing at the Goody's Headache 500 in Bristol. He was consistent, but Terry Labonte was even more so. Labonte had retaken the points lead, with Gordon right behind in second place. Dale Earnhardt kept driving through the pain and was a gutsy third.

The fall season looked interesting.

"Booooo!"

"And in the number 24 Chevy Monte Carlo, Jeff Gordon!"
"Booooo!"
"Get him off the track!"
"Spoiled kid!"
"Get him out of here!"

The Gordon-haters had been building for months, as Jeff's success kept rising. The animosity reached a new crescendo at the Mountain Dew Southern 500 in Darlington on the first day of September, 1996. Many NASCAR fans had children older than Jeff, and they didn't like the fact that this young guy was in the running for a second straight Winston Cup championship. Though Gordon was receiving his share of cheers, he also had the largest outpouring of boos, by far.

Booing by detractors is something Jeff and his family have had to get used to. *Stock-car Racing* magazine described one crowd's reaction to Jeff as a response "that seems more appropriate for a serial killer, convicted felon, or drug dealer than for someone whose only offense is doing everything right."

Some of these spiteful motorheads (slang for NASCAR fans) might be chagrined to know that Gordon once *aspired* to their catcalls. Gordon's mom Carol told me how, back in the early 1980s, when she and Jeff were watching Steve Kinser tear up the sprint tracks, Carol became irritated at how frequently Kinser was booed. It prompted her to ask, "Why do they do that, Jeff? There isn't anybody better out there, so why do they boo him?"

Jeff answered, "Mom, that's *why* they boo him—because he *is* the best. They're always rooting for the underdog. I hope they boo me like that someday."

"His wishes have come true," Carol laughs.

It's a burden that ultimately affects Gordon's entire family. For example, in January of 1998, Carol was at a blackjack table in Reno, Nevada, with her good friends Steve and Linda. Later, a pit boss came by wearing a Kellogg's racing tie, and when the dealer saw the tie she said, "Hey, Terry Labonte is my kid's favorite driver."

Steve said, "Oh, you follow Winston Cup racing?"

Carol told me she immediately kicked Steve under the table and leaned over, whispering, "Do not—*do not* tell them who I am."

The dealer then started talking about Winston Cup drivers and eventually worked her way to Jeff Gordon.

Then Linda said, "Hey, before you really put your foot in your mouth, you should know that this is Jeff's mom."

The dealer was understandably taken aback, so she tried to defend herself. "Can I explain why I feel the way I do? The problem is, he's just too good. He's too good-looking, got too much money, and had too much success at such a young age."

"So that's a reason to dislike somebody?" Carol asked. "Aren't you a parent?"

"Yeah," the dealer admitted.

"Do you want your children to be successful in life?"

"Well, yes."

"That's all I ever wanted for my kids," Carol said.

Other NASCAR followers are "getting it" even without having the benefit of running up against Jeff's mom. One motorhead wrote a letter to the weekly *NASCAR Winston Cup Scene* (September 10, 1998): "I have been a Dale Earnhardt fan since I can remember. And yes, while attending races at Pocono and Dover for the past three years, I booed Jeff Gordon just like many others. It was fun!

"Then I took a good look at this young man, his driving, his crew, et cetera, and I said to myself, 'What, am I crazy? I am seeing history made. Enjoy!'"

Another Winston Cup attendee felt that Jeff's consistent success had taken the fun out of the contests. "Any sport where one contestant wins 37.5 percent of the events doesn't deserve my support."

But NASCAR knows Gordon is good for Winston Cup racing. NASCAR president Bill France likes to point out the obvious: Jeff Gordon puts people in the seats. Some of them come to boo him. Others come to cheer him. However, everyone who comes *pays to do it.*

Most important, Jeff has come to terms with the crowd's reaction. "How can I complain when people boo?" he told Shav Glick of the *Los Angeles Times.* "Actually, it's a good thing because it means I'm winning. If I wasn't winning, you wouldn't hear any of that, so like I say, how can I complain? I'm not bothered by it, really. I just kind of smile, wave back at them, and walk away."

So Gordon didn't flinch as his car got ready for the start of the Mountain Dew Southern 500 in Darlington, South Carolina, on September 1. The people's favorite for this day was clearly Dale Jarrett. Here he had the chance to become the second driver ever to claim the "Winston Million," at that time given to any driver who won three of four select Winston Cup races: the most prestigious race (Daytona 500), the fastest race (the Winston Select 500 at Talladega), the longest race (now called the Coca-Cola 600), and the oldest race (the Southern 500 in Darlington). Bill Elliott was the first (and only, so far) driver to accomplish the feat, taking home his seven-figure check in 1985.

Confidence in the Jarrett camp was running high. When the owner of Jarrett's car said he had given his driver the best vehicle he had ever built, Gordon offered, "That means he's got a guided missile."

Dale Jarrett agreed with Gordon's assessment. Journalist Paul Hemphill caught him saying he did think he had the best car, and even wondered what a driver like Jeff could do in it. "There's no telling what Jeff Gordon . . . could run in this car," he said. "But it's mine, and he's not getting it."

Jarrett's pursuit of the million was short-lived. He was in the lead, running strong, when an amateur-style driver and car (the car itself was sponsored by a pickle grower and probably nobody was more surprised than the driver himself when he actually qualified) started leaking trace amounts of oil. Jarrett's tires spun out and sent him into the wall.

The race went on. (The motorheads who booed must have been saying, "Oh, no, we paid our money to watch the Kid win again?")

Then, with about sixty laps to go, the race got very interesting. A little-known driver named Hut Stricklin managed to slip by Gordon. Suddenly, it was a three-man race between Gordon, Stricklin, and Martin, with Stricklin out in the lead.

The crowd got into it; NASCAR fans especially love the underdog, and Stricklin became the most-loved man in all of South Carolina for a fierce sixty laps.

The bad guy that day? Number 24, Jeff Gordon.

But the race wasn't over, and a race has to be won with a team. Stricklin's car started misbehaving—it was getting dangerously overheated—and the would-be giant-slayer cast a wary eye at his temperature gauge.

In the end, Gordon got a great draft, punched it at just the right time, and Stricklin was history. Jeff rode the lead all the way to the finish line and claimed his seventh win of the season.

Scorching September

The next week, at the Miller Genuine Draft 400 in Richmond, Gordon started at number two and finished at number two. More important for the series championship, Labonte came in fifth, leaving Jeff just 4 points out of the lead.

The number 24 team then made a trip up north for the MBNA 500 in Dover, Delaware. NASCAR and Ivy League college names are rarely uttered in the same sentence, but the Rainbow Warriors' success had not gone unnoticed by the academic elite. Jeff and Ray Evernham were asked to address a freshman engineering class at Princeton University in New Jersey. Though Ray has hired some of the most-educated engineers in the business, neither he nor Jeff has a college degree, which meant that of all the people in the room, the two least academically accredited men were the ones lecturing.

Perhaps flush with the esteem granted them, Evernham and Gordon rewarded the Ivy Leaguers for their confidence by pulling in a first-place finish on Sunday.

Now back in the points lead, number 24 fans were talking a repeat championship, but Gordon worked to quash speculation. He didn't need the pressure, and he thought it way too early to look that far ahead in the season.

"There's still plenty of races to go," he explained. "Anything can happen. We're just gonna think about doing our job and doing the best job that we can. That's what we did today, and it paid off."

On September 22, 1996, Jeff qualified tenth for the Goody's Headache Powder 500 in Martinsville, Virginia. With the season heading to the end, each race took on momentous importance. There were six races left, and Jeff led Terry Labonte by just 76 points.

The following week, Jeff did it again, winning the Tyson Holly Farms 400, the last NASCAR race to be run at the aging North Wilkesboro track. Jeff was pumped up (nothing unusual there) as he recognized the NASCAR history he was making. Not only had he won the inaugural Brickyard 400—something for which he'll always be remembered—but now he had taken home the last win at North Wilkesboro.

September had been a scorching month. In its five races Gordon chalked up four wins and one second-place finish—an almost superhuman feat by NASCAR standards. He kept pulling away from Labonte—leading now by 111 points—and was the clear favorite to win it all for the second year in a row with just four races left in the season. All he had to do was keep finishing in the top-ten and the championship would be his, almost regardless of how Labonte performed.

But NASCAR racing is never quite that simple.

The Fall

Autumn 1996 was the fall for car number 24 in more ways than one. With more than a 100-point lead, Jeff's grip on the championship was firm. However, Gordon's luck began to run out at exactly the wrong time. Jeff led early at the UAW-GM Quality 500 in Charlotte, but then struggled to maintain his position near the front. On lap 176 he was in third place, but fans started buzzing when they saw him pull off the track for what seemed like an untimely pit stop. His car was overheating. The Rainbow Warriors lifted the hood and literally tried to drown the heat out of the engine. They got him back out, but the stop cost Jeff dearly—three laps, to be precise— and he ended with a paltry thirty-first-place finish.

To make matters worse, Labonte finally won a race. It was just Labonte's second win of the season and his first win ever (in thirty-seven career starts) at Charlotte. Combined with Jeff's poor showing, the win pulled Labonte within one point of the Kid. Terry was now doing more than breathing down Gordon's neck; he was practically climbing inside his car.

The next week at Rockingham, the number 24 team had a chance to keep from collapsing. They were still in the lead, after all. Surely they wouldn't finish thirty-first again.

They didn't. They finished twelfth.

Labonte finished third.

And Gordon lost his points lead.

Two races to go for the 1996 season.

Jeff was 32 points behind Terry Labonte, but Terry showed up for the Slick Fifty 500 in Phoenix with a cast on the forefinger of his driving hand.

He had broken it during a practice earlier in the week when his gas pedal stuck and he crashed into the wall. His team fixed him up with a splint and wired his hand to an electrical stimulus. They also got him a smaller steering wheel.

And Gordon was having troubles of his own. Number 24 just couldn't settle down, and handled poorly the entire week. Of course, the frequent sandstorms (that's right—*sandstorms!*) didn't help that much, and Jeff qualified nineteenth. He finished a much better fifth, but Labonte did him two better, coming in third.

With one race remaining, Jeff now trailed Terry by forty-seven points, and the outlook was grim. If Labonte could finish in the top eight—something he had done in all but seven of the thirty races he had run in 1996—the title was his. Gordon could squeeze in with the laps bonuses and a first-place finish—provided Labonte came in no higher than ninth.

Gordon was just thirteen years old when Labonte won his first Winston Cup championship in 1984 (for which he was paid a relatively paltry $150,000—compared to the more than $1.5 million payout that awaited the winner in 1996).

Gordon said to journalist Paul Hemphill, "I didn't even know what Winston Cup was at that age. I knew what the Daytona 500 and the Indianapolis 500 were. I was racing go-carts and getting ready to make the move to sprint cars. I was always racing on Sundays, so I didn't get a chance to watch Winston Cup."

Now, of course, he'd be able to do more than watch. In fact, he'd have the second-best seat in the house—the outside pole.

Gordon qualified second for the last race of the year in Atlanta, ominously sandwiched between the two Labontes. Paul Hemphill caught Gordon talking on the radio just seconds before the race began: "It's a great day," Jeff told Ray Evernham. "God's on our side. I can feel it."

But less than ten laps into the race, the Rainbow Warriors were frozen with panic when they heard Jeff cry out, "The brakes are gone; the brakes are gone!" His car was shaking all over the place.

It seemed like an eternity (but it was only seconds) until the brakes stabilized and Jeff was able to maneuver his vehicle into the pits. It turned out the left wheel was loose. Gordon sat in his car, waiting for the work to be done, while Terry chased after the title with vengeance.

Terry had already passed his younger brother Bobby and picked up bonus points for leading a lap, which meant that he could now virtually clinch the title with just a tenth-place finish. Evernham's crew had a near-flawless pit, all things considered, but even so, Gordon came out of it two laps down.

But Gordon focused on the task at hand and displayed extra fine driving that day. Gordon finished third—not shabby for being two laps down early on—but Terry won the title. Jeff immediately radioed Terry's crew: "Congratulations, guys, you did it."

In the postrace comments, Jeff showed his spunk to the reporters: "You better watch out. It might be one-two-three next year for Hendrick Motorsports."

Once Again—The Dominator

Though Jeff finished second in the Winston Cup standings for the year, his dominance was clear. Both Labonte and Gordon had thirty-one starts, twenty-one top-five finishes, and twenty-four top-ten finishes, but the similarities ended there. Labonte won two races to Gordon's ten. The second-highest race winner was Rusty Wallace with five wins, but Wallace had only eight top-five finishes (and ended up seventh in the overall standings).

Again NASCAR rewards consistency over brilliance. One thing was clear, however. Gordon and the Rainbow Warriors had proven that 1995 was no fluke; number 24 would never be taken for granted again.

When you put 1995 together with 1996, the picture becomes even more impressive. Jeff won seventeen races out of a total of sixty-two—that's more than one-fourth of all races, and more than the number of wins garnered by the next two drivers *combined*. And as for winning money, in 1996 Gordon earned over $500,000 more than his champion teammate Terry Labonte—$2,484,518 to $1,939,213. Certainly he'd rather have the trophy, but . . .

In early December, at the awards banquet, Jeff became the first recipient of the True Value Man of the Year award. This prize was inaugurated in 1996 to honor drivers involved in charity work. "The neatest thing about [the award] was the surprise," Gordon writes on his Internet Web site. "You know, you have no idea. Then they announced it at the banquet and I was just blown away. Because you see what a lot of these other guys do out there in the sport and the support they give different fundraisers and charities. That's almost more important than a lot of other things we do out there."

Meanwhile, however, serious troubles were brewing for Ray Hendrick's team. Shortly before the banquet, the NASCAR world learned that what had been only whispered about in the spring was coming true: Rick Hendrick was being indicted by a federal grand jury on allegations of money laundering, conspiracy, and mail fraud. An investigation of American Honda (Hendrick is the country's largest Honda dealer) reportedly resulted in twenty bribery and corruption charges.

A federal prosecutor alleged that Hendrick had been able to import cars that other dealers couldn't touch because he had supposedly made large payments to top Honda salespeople—in one case, even helping a salesperson buy two homes. According to Shaun Assael, author of *Wide Open* (1998), and widely reported news accounts, Hendrick admitted making payments to salespeople, but insisted that the payments had not been bribes, as nothing was expected in return. The matter would have to be settled in court.

Hendrick had gone out of his way to cooperate with investigators, and the NASCAR world—a close-knit bunch, to be sure—seemed to take it personally when the indictment came down just days before Hendrick's moment in glory: his second straight championship banquet.

When Hendrick was finally introduced at the awards banquet, the thousand-plus people in the room literally erupted with a sustained and ear-splitting standing ovation that raised goose bumps on people's necks. Hendrick was so overcome by the moment and the show of support that he had to pause before making it to the podium.

But early 1997 would bring more dire news for the Hendrick team.

chapter 17

Stunning Start: February—May 1997

"With three Hendrick cars behind you, you ain't got a chance."
—NASCAR competitor Bill Elliott, 1997

Rick Hendrick and his wife, Linda, had kept a secret from the NASCAR world for several weeks, but early in 1997, the ominous news was announced: Hendrick had contracted a particularly pernicious kind of leukemia that typically kills half of those afflicted within four to six years of diagnosis.

The public knew it was serious when Hendrick missed the Daytona 500 on February 16; he was so weakened by the disease, the prescription drugs, and aggressive treatments that he wasn't strong enough to leave his house.

Overnight, Hendrick cars sported the legend, "1-800-Marrow-2." This was part of the Racing Against Leukemia Drive, which has led to tens of thousands of phone calls and several donor matches for the National Marrow Donor Program.

Thanks to Jeff Gordon, the phone number would receive great exposure.

Destiny in Daytona

Jeff had three goals going into the 1997 racing season. His first goal, not surprisingly, was to win the Winston Cup championship. His second goal was to win a road race. His third goal was to win the most prestigious race of all—the Daytona 500.

Daytona is everything to NASCAR drivers. Darrell Waltrip explained it to journalist Paul Hemphill: "Our sport is Daytona. It's got to be on your resumé. It's like the Super Bowl, the World Series, the U.S. Open. I've won eighty-four races, but that wouldn't mean anything if I hadn't won Daytona."

Waltrip's sentiment is echoed by most in the sport. Terry Labonte has said, "Ask any driver in the garage area and they will tell you if they had just one race to win, the Daytona 500 would be the one."

If it was possible for anyone to want to win Daytona more than Gordon did, it would have to be Dale Earnhardt. Despite being called the greatest stock-car driver ever by a NASCAR-appointed panel of experts, Earnhardt had never won Daytona, even though he has told reporters, "The Daytona 500 is the granddaddy of them all."

It took Jeff fifty-seven laps to take the lead, but he held the position for over thirty laps. He was bumped back to third but was still running strong when disaster struck. Jeff cut a tire on lap 110 and had to bring the number 24 car in, even though the rest of the field was running under a green. The dejected driver rolled into the pit, lamenting to his crew chief, "I've just cost us the race."

"I thought this was going to be another Daytona 500 where I just rode around and finished the thing," the champ recalled later.

But Ray and the Rainbow Warriors weren't ready to concede anything. In a furious rush they pulled off a stellar pit stop. When the jack man dropped Jeff back down, Jeff punched the accelerator and sped out of the pit.

Mark Martin, leading the race, was charging fast, eager to put Jeff a lap down. He didn't make it. Jeff squeezed his Rainbow car on to the track in front of him. He was last in the field, but still on the lead lap. The Rainbow Warriors cheered.

Now it was up to Gordon.

Number 24 got a break twelve laps later when a yellow flag allowed Jeff to catch up with the rest of the field. (The leaders aren't allowed to pass a pace car that runs about 55 mph, which makes everyone in the back of the field bunch up.) Gordon was still near the back, but no longer in danger of being lapped. After the restart, Jeff slowly and methodically worked his way back near the front, ready to strike when the opportunity presented itself.

That opportunity came on lap 189. The three Hendrick teammates—Gordon, Terry Labonte, and Ricky Craven—were several cars behind Earnhardt, who was running second, and Bill Elliott, who was running first.

Dale Earnhardt got too high coming out of turn two and just barely scraped the wall. The slight bump slowed him down enough so that when Jarrett and Irvan came around they plowed into Earnhardt from behind, sending him careening off the track with multiple rollovers.

Once again, Earnhardt's Daytona dreams were dashed.

But Jeff's lived on, and now the three Hendrick teammates were the primary pursuers of Bill Elliott in his number 94 McDonald's Ford Thunderbird. Gordon was feeling good. "I'm sitting there on the restart," he recounted after the race, "and I've got Bill Elliott in front of me and my two teammates sitting behind me. That was a sign. A good sign."

The reason it was so important for Jeff to have his teammates with him is explained by *Sports Illustrated*'s Ed Hinton in its February 24, 1997, issue. "During the preceding week's qualifying and preliminary races, the word had been that as a result of NASCAR's new rules on rear spoilers and body-work, some mysterious aerodynamics had come into play. Drivers needed more help—from two or more cars—to create a draft, to 'push' them when they made a run at passing another car. At precisely the time Gordon needed such aid the most, up came his stablemates, Labonte and Craven."

Elliott was horrified when he realized what was behind him. "I was dead meat, and I knew it," he said. "It was just a matter of when and where."

According to Hinton, with the Daytona 500 just six laps from the finish, Gordon called Labonte on the radio. "Terry," he said, "it would be pretty neat if we could get these three Hendrick cars by Elliott."

Terry quickly agreed. "Yeah, that'd be neat. I'll be with you."

With Labonte on board, Gordon switched over to Ricky's channel and checked the situation with Craven. "Terry's going with me," he said. "Who you going with?"

Craven shot back, "I'm going with you."

That settled, Gordon went to work, virtually jet-propelled by his team-mates. "I had a ton of momentum from Terry and Ricky," he said later.

Elliott's nightmare came true. Gordon slipped by him, immediately followed by the zooming Labonte and Craven.

Gordon's elation was checked somewhat shortly after the race when he saw Earnhardt's mangled car (with a destroyed rear and crushed right side) wobble down the straightaway. Ever the competitor, number 3 was determined to salvage what few points he could, as long as he didn't have to push his car across the finish line.

Gordon needn't have worried. Earnhardt saw him drive by, then flipped him a thumbs-up, followed by an "I'm okay" sign.

After rolling into the pits, Jeff got on a cell phone, still in his car, and dialed Rick Hendrick. "This one is for you!" he shouted.

Ray also had his fun. "Hey, boss," he told Hendrick, "you said all we had to do was finish one-two-three in the Daytona 500. What's my next job?"

Hendrick, gravely ill but still fully alive, quipped, "You're gonna have to run the car dealerships."

What a day it must have been for Rick! The all-Hendrick sweep was the first time ever that a team took the first three spots in a major race. To do it at the Daytona 500, the most prestigious race there is, was almost too good to be true.

Jeff willingly shared the winner's circle with his two teammates. After the race, Gordon told Hinton, "It didn't matter which of us finished first, second, or third, so long as we finished one-two-three for Rick."

"This is the best medicine that the good Lord can give me right now," Hendrick said.

It was destiny at Daytona for Gordon, a great, great win in a career that seemed unstoppable. Afterward Jeff reflected, "I don't think I'll ever have a bigger thrill than when I won the Daytona 500, not only because we had won the biggest race there is, but because it meant so much to Rick. . . . It was just so great to know what our winning meant to him. It couldn't have been a more emotional moment." Jeff's name was the twenty-fifth to be engraved on the Harley J. Early Daytona 500 trophy. He was the youngest champion ever, knocking out Richard Petty for that honor.

Jeff's winning car is at the Hendrick Museum. You can still see the rubber marks—practically covering up the 4 in 24—where drivers rubbed against Jeff to congratulate him on his win.

Just a few weeks after the Daytona victory, Jeff had one of those mind-blowing experiences that tell a person he's definitely famous. Gordon went out to his mailbox and pulled out a letter addressed simply to "Jeff Gordon, Race-car Driver."

He had come quite a way since his family had moved to Pittsboro.

Slip-Sliding Away

How do you top a debut victory at Daytona? By winning two races in a row!

It didn't look like it would be Jeff's day early on. Jarrett was all over the lead at the Goodwrench Service 400 in Rockingham, practically claiming it as his own. He led an astonishing 323 of the first 350 laps, but in NASCAR, while leading the most laps will get a driver 5 bonus points, it's being out in front at the finish line that earns the coveted 175 points.

In the end Jeff became the first driver in over a decade to win the first two races in a season.

A tough race the next week in Richmond brought Jeff home in fourth place—behind three Fords—but still leading the points race. He lost the points lead the next week in Hampton, Virginia, during the early laps of the Primestar 500. Jeff heard "a huge rumbling" and "an explosion" under his hood. Fans watched as Jeff drove behind the pit wall. A forty-second-place finish dropped Jeff to fourth in the standings. But there was still a lot of racing to do in 1997.

Gordon came back with a strong third-place finish at Darlington two weeks later, once again trailing the Fords, but his momentum was stalled at Roanoke, Texas, in the Interstate Batteries 500. It was the first race at the Texas Motor Speedway, built by Bruton Smith, the legendary track owner, CEO, and chairman of the board of Speedway Motorsports.

The event was getting near the halfway mark when Ernie Irvan crashed right in front of Jeff. The Rainbow car spun into pit road and had to be hauled into the garage for repairs. Gordon was able to get back into the race, but he was out of the running for a victory. His thirtieth-place finish dropped him another notch, to fifth place, in the Winston Cup standings.

The Rainbow Warriors were determined not to let Jeff slip any farther in the standings. They wanted a strong run the next week at Bristol.

And they got it.

Winning Ways

Jeff qualified fifth for the April 13 running of the Food City 500 in Bristol. He ran near the front most of the day, ultimately leading 125 of the race's 500 laps.

Gordon had his hands full just trying not to lose second place to Terry Labonte. The Kellogg's car was right there, ready to move, and Jeff felt pinned. When the white flag (signifying the last lap) dropped, Gordon figured he didn't have the car to catch Rusty Wallace in a single lap, so he focused on maintaining second. (Race cars can be very temperamental in their performance. Expert drivers can tell when the car they are operating simply isn't fast enough to catch someone else. That's why you'll sometimes hear crew chiefs say, "We had about a tenth-place car today." That means even if the driver had run a brilliant race, his car wasn't fast enough to allow him to win it.)

Then Jeff spotted some lapped cars up ahead and said to himself, *Man, if they hold him up, I might have a chance.*

All of a sudden, Gordon had his sights set on first place. Wallace did get held up, just slightly, but even more importantly, Jeff seemed to fly out of the second turn. In a heartbeat, he was right on Wallace's bumper.

Jeff hung in there, waiting for Wallace to make a mistake. Rusty didn't—not really, anyway, just a slight wobble with a loose car—but that gave Jeff enough room to move up and do a little bumping going into turn three.

The two cars rubbed through the entire turn four and then again coming out of it. Both drivers were determined to take the checkered flag, but number 24 broke through the line first.

In *Portrait of a Champion,* Jeff recalls, "That was probably the most excited I've ever been after a finish because my adrenaline was flowing and it came right down to that final corner. . . ."

The next week in Martinsville, Virginia, Jeff started from fourth place, but soon showed the field that Ray and company had given him the car to beat. Today number 24 was running fast. Gordon wrestled the lead away on lap 21, and wouldn't relinquish it for over three hundred miles.

Though Jeff lost the lead (Bobby Hamilton squeezed through and took over), he was elated to still be in the running after spinning out. "Guys," he yelled over the radio, "it's getting wild!"

Finally, on lap 376, Jeff started to move near the start/finish line. Going into turn one, he got inside and established a line, and it was all over for Hamilton.

Jeff had the lead back, and he held on to it through the checkered flag.

After a Talladega, Alabama, competition that made news because it was run without a single caution (Jeff placed fifth), and a Sonoma, California, race in which Jeff qualified third and placed second, the Rainbow Warriors unveiled a new, red car at the Winston on May 17 to promote Jurassic Park: The Ride at Universal Studios in Florida. Jeff had a dinosaur on the back of his uniform and on the hood of his car, but it didn't take the competition long to learn that this nonpoints race wasn't about to be a joyride. Jeff and Ray were taking it seriously, and the car looked fast—too fast, as it turned out in qualification, as Jeff was penalized for speeding on pit road and given the last starting position (nineteenth).

But that just showcased how dynamite the car really was. Jeff got the win, and it was celebrated with firecrackers booming out in the Charlotte night.

If the Jurassic Park ride proved to be half as good as the car that promoted it, theme-park visitors would get their money's worth—and more.

Spoiling the Party

It was only a matter of time until NASCAR figured: If you can't beat him, give the other guys a boost! The normally mild-mannered Ray Evernham finally spoke out about what he believed was a drastically unfair ruling that gave Ford cars a decided advantage over Jeff's Chevy. With Hendrick Motorsports Chevys winning the championship two years in a row, and NASCAR worshiping at the altar of parity, NASCAR added a quarter-inch to the rear spoilers on the Ford Thunderbirds. A larger rear spoiler gives a car more down-force right where it needs it most—over the back tires. This gives the car better traction, which means faster speeds.

Ray pointed to tests showing that Fords already had more horsepower and down-force, which led him to conclude that NASCAR was trying to give Ford a hand up since they couldn't win on a level playing field.

"This is not about making the cars equal," Ray argued, according to biographer George Mair in his book, *Natural Born Winner*. "This is like putting twenty-pound ankle weights on Michael Jordan. . . . Ford is admitting that on an equal basis they can't beat Hendrick Motorsports."

NASCAR and the competition would eventually learn a lesson: Don't get Ray riled. He doesn't just get mad. He gets even.

By winning.

Jeff took his DuPont car with Pepsi stickers to the Coca-Cola 600 in Charlotte on May 25. Gordon had once enjoyed an endorsement contract with Coke, but the classic soda opted to use him on a regional basis only (around the South). Pepsi saw Jeff's national potential and Jeff joined the Next Generation, suddenly popping up on Pepsi machines and in commercials aired across the United States.

Jeff qualified first with a record speed of 184.3 mph, which was something of an anomaly for 1997. Jeff had captured nine poles in his 1995 championship season, then won just over half that (five) in 1996. In 1997, the Concord (North Carolina) track would give Jeff not just his first, but his only pole of the year.

During the warm-up lap, Jeff felt great. "When I ran through [turn] four just before the green, I said, 'Oh, yeah! This car's gonna be good!'"

It was a late, 6:40 P.M. start, and the asphalt was so soft from the day's heat that the tires weren't gripping well. The Rainbow Warriors, by Jeff's instructions, set the number 24 car to oversteer. This caused the rear end to skid slightly during turns early on, but the thinking was that, as the evening wore on and the track cooled, the looser setup would give Jeff a better grip for the all-important last laps. "I want the car to be just right after dark," Gordon explained to a reporter from *Sports Illustrated* (August 18, 1997).

Immediately after the start, Hendrick teammate Ricky Craven came up on the outside. On the inside, Dale Jarrett's Thunderbird, a haze of red and blue, was waiting to strike.

Gordon let both Jarrett and Craven pass him, then tucked himself right behind them. "You get right back on the guy who passed you and show him what it was like when he was behind you."

The maneuver allowed Jeff to retake the lead just a few laps later. Jeff was running well until he experienced a freak pit accident at lap 54.

A tire rolled against the jack handle and released it prematurely. The number 24 car slipped off the jack, partially damaging the body on the left side of the car. It was obvious the car needed repairs, but neither Jeff nor Ray wanted to go down a lap so the Rainbow car sped back on to the track just in time to beat the pace car.

Ray brought Jeff back in on the next lap for repairs. By the time the green flag dropped, number 24 was all the way back in thirty-eighth place with an extremely loose car. The race was still young, though, and Jeff had over four hundred miles to work his way back up front—but his car was still very difficult to handle.

Fortunately, Gordon doesn't need a perfect car. He's a good-enough driver to get most anything near the front, and shortly after he passed Earnhardt to lay claim to sixth place, he got a call from Evernham.

"The rain's coming," Ray said.

The words were more ominous than you might think. After two hundred laps—three hundred miles—the race would become official. Jeff was driving on lap 180, which meant the race could be over in just twenty more laps.

It was time for Gordon to go all-out, loose car or no.

Almost immediately, another vehicle wrecked in turn four—where the wrecks usually happen at Concord—and a caution flag came out. That gave the Rainbow Warriors another opportunity to work Jeff's car back into shape. Back out on the track, Jeff drove fast, trying to beat the rain, but the weather came on even harder than he did. On lap 195—five laps before it otherwise would have been official—the race was stopped with Jeff running in third place behind Bobby Labonte and Ernie Irvan.

The rain delay persisted for two and a half hours. Race teams were informed that the cars would race for another hour (until 12:45 A.M.), then run an additional twenty laps.

Labonte got a huge jump on the restart. For the next hundred laps or so, Jeff ran near the front. He took his last pit on lap 296. The Rainbow Warriors gave him four new tires and twenty-two gallons of gas and still managed to get him out in third place, behind Rusty Wallace and Jeff Burton.

With new tires, Jeff felt confident. He pulled behind Burton and let the air rattle his rival. Burton felt his car sliding and let his rival by.

Now there was just Wallace, who, Gordon was informed, had pitted twenty laps before Jeff, so his tires would have far less grip—meaning that Jeff could now have a lot of fun stealing this guy's air!

With seventeen laps to go, Jeff made his move, practically crawling up underneath Wallace's rear bumper. When Wallace's T-Bird skated out, Jeff passed Wallace on the outside.

Rusty stayed calm and slipped in right behind Gordon, hoping to return the favor. Jeff's hopes to blow right by didn't quite turn out. Now *he* was the hunted, with plenty of race left. Jeff rode high and wide to protect his lead. That gave Wallace an opportunity to dive down for an inside pass. For a split second, the Rainbow Warriors held their breath until it became apparent that Wallace's last gasp would come up short.

It was late, almost one A.M., when Jeff crossed the finish line in first place. Ray proved that he and Jeff could find a way to win even when NASCAR seemingly gave the Fords favored treatment.

chapter 18

Inside the Car at Long Pond

"When you need a yellow bad, you'll 'bout say anything to try and get one."

—Jeff Gordon, 1997

What's it like to be Jeff Gordon on race day? A *Details* magazine reporter traveled to Long Pond, Pennsylvania, for the Pocono 500 on June 8, 1997, and captured some of Jeff's pre-race rituals while also giving his readers an inside view (in the September 1997 issue) of what happens between a driver and crew chief during a typical race.

On this day, Jeff's breakfast was pretty mild, especially considering the long day that lay ahead: Raisin Bran, a banana, and vitamins. After breakfast, Jeff drove a simulated lap of the Pocono racetrack on a computer, grumbling all the while that the game didn't include gear-shifting. His time was 56.344 seconds.

"Is that good?" Jeff asked, but his question was met with silence.

Gordon then had to fulfill his obligations—first to his sponsors and reps (the usual handshaking, small talk, and photographers), then to NASCAR (the weekly drivers' meeting where officials go over last-minute details), and then to God (chapel service).

The *Details* writer, David Handelman, asked Jeff about this last visit.

"[Faith] helps me be content with whatever happens out on the track," Jeff said. "Last week I ran into the back of a guy. I questioned, 'Could I have prevented that?' Certain things you can learn from and be able to change. But some things you can't."

Every race, Brooke writes out a Bible verse or hymn lyrics, which are placed on the dashboard. For this race Brooke chose a popular chorus: "Our God is an awesome God/He reigns from Heaven above/With wisdom, power and love/Our God is an awesome God."

Pennsylvania can be hot in June, and the temperature in Jeff's car will eventually reach 120 degrees. Over the next five hours, Gordon will sweat away up to fifteen pounds—which helps to explain his post-race habit of gorging on filling foods.

Though Gordon had qualified eleventh, he soon worked his way up to third place, where he tucked behind a driver who doesn't normally lead: Greg Sacks. Jeff brought his car up close, stole Sacks' air, and just as Jeff broke to steer his car down into the inner curve, Sacks spun out of control.

Immediately Jeff got on the radio: "Is Sacks okay?" he asked Ray.

"He's getting out of the car," Evernham assured him.

After the race, Handelman, the *Details* reporter, asked Gordon about this, and about how he handles the startling statistic that the average Winston Cup driver gets in about seven accidents a season. "I love what I do," Gordon shrugged. "I know the risk. If it happens to me, it happens."

Still, Handelman, clearly in awe, presses on. "If, say, Tiger Woods breaks concentration and misses a birdie," Handelman writes, "it merely costs him a stroke. If Jeff Gordon hesitates for a millisecond of reaction time, he may be carried off on a stretcher."

Evernham explains to the reporter that Gordon's driving skills are really a "conditioned response." "He doesn't even know he knows it." You don't really have time to think; you just react."

It didn't take long for Jeff to punch his car into the lead after he wrestled second place away from Sacks, but his lead was short-lived.

"Uh, Ray," Jeff said over the radio, "I don't know if I got a flat right rear."

Evernham's attention was riveted on the track as he waited for Jeff to pass so he could get a good look (using binoculars) at the tire. Ray didn't see any signs of a flat, and since bringing Jeff in on a green would put him a lap down, he left it up to his driver. "Looks all right to me. If that thing's real bad, let's get it in here."

Jeff gave it up after one more revolution. The car was just too shaky, so he came in for an unscheduled pit and took on four new tires. Jeff fell from first to last in about twenty seconds, and the new leader was coming hard around turn four, ready to put Jeff a lap down. Jeff hit the accelerator and made it back out on the lead lap, but near the back.

That's when the *Details* reporter noticed something curious. Brooke immediately left the infield parking lot to watch the race on TV. "When he's in back and has to fight his way to the front, it makes me nervous," she explained.

Meanwhile, Ray's attention was focused on the suspicious tire. "Good call," he told Jeff over the radio. "You had a puncture."

It was only a matter of time until the other drivers had to start pitting and that helped push him back up to seventh place. However, as the race wore on, Jeff needed to pit again, and he was out-of-sync with the other drivers. Another pit on a green would put him right back in last place.

Such is the angst of being a crew chief; all he can do in this situation is cross his fingers and pray for a caution.

Jeff decided to do a little more than pray. Before too long, Evernham's radio crackled with Jeff's voice. "I think there's something on the track on turn one," he said. "I'm hearing stuff under the tires."

After a few more laps, Gordon added, "It might be a piece of brake rotor."

Evernham sent someone to tell the NASCAR officials what Jeff was feeling, but they've heard it all before—and then some. It's not unheard-of for a driver who wants a caution to "imagine" track debris. After NASCAR looked over the area and got back to Evernham, Ray radioed back the bad news: "Everybody's reporting debris, but they're not doing anything about it."

Later Jeff would say to Handelman, "When you need a yellow [flag] bad, you'll 'bout say anything to try and get one."

While Jeff's scouting failed, perhaps the prayer worked—at least for Jeff. Just when things were starting to look dire, Bobby Labonte skidded along a wall and tore the right front fender off his car. NASCAR couldn't ignore this.

Jeff finally got his yellow flag.

"All right," Evernham screamed in delight. "This is gonna save our butts!"

The caution put Jeff back in schedule with the other cars' pits, allowing him to focus on what he does best—racing. By lap 79, he was in second place, and fifty tough laps later, another crash gave the Rainbow Warriors a chance to send Jeff out in first place. He hung on to win the race by a formidable 1.4 seconds.

In the postrace interviews, Gordon was quick to thank higher powers. "The Lord was on our side today," he told a radio host.

It's easy to get the impression God was on his side for more than a single day. Through this June 8 race (and counting the nonpoints Winston race), Jeff had won an amazing 50 percent of all Winston Cup races in 1997.

But that still wasn't enough to satisfy either Jeff or Ray. "Wins are fun and enjoyable," Jeff said, "but it's the championship you really want."

chapter 19

Guts and Glory: June—November 1997

"When you have a year like we had, if we hadn't finished it off by winning the championship, it would have been very disappointing. It was a year that was meant for a championship."

—Jeff Gordon, 1997

The NASCAR gods seemed determined to remind people that Jeff was a mere mortal the next week at Michigan on June 15, 1997. Jeff was practicing on the Michigan Speedway on Saturday when he came up too high and crashed into the wall, pretty much demolishing his car's right front end, puncturing a tire, and buckling the hood. The car, *Bob,* was a sorry mess and had to be retired.

The Rainbow Warriors knew there would be little sleep that night, as they had less than twenty-four hours to get a new car ready to race. It wasn't the strongest, and Jeff finished fifth.

Roger Penske's California Speedway in Fontana opened up one week later for its inaugural race, the California 500 by NAPA. Jeff started near the front, but bided his time for two dozen laps before taking the lead. Everyone chased the DuPont car for a good seventy laps until Dale Jarrett, and then Terry Labonte, took over. After a hard day's driving, Jeff was back in the lead, but his gas supply was nearly exhausted.

It was close—real close—but Jeff's car made it. He said in his photo essay that the final lap "was probably the slowest lap I made all day long. . . . I learned a lot about how to save and conserve fuel and win a race in a different fashion."

The win in California kept Jeff at the top of the Winston Cup standings, but two consecutive poor showings, at Daytona Beach and Loudon (twenty-first and twenty-third respectively), put Terry Labonte back on top.

The next week at Pocono (Pennsylvania), Jeff radioed Ray with sober news—he thought he needed a pit to take care of a flat or punctured tire. Ray watched Jeff pass and didn't see anything wrong, so he told Jeff to stay out there, figuring that maybe Gordon had just picked up some rubber or debris that was making the car difficult to handle. Tires get pretty hot, so it's not unusual for track debris to stick to them when a car runs over something.

"Find a different groove," Ray advised.

Jeff did, the car came back to him, and Ray saved Jeff ten positions or more by avoiding an unnecessary pit stop.

Winston Cup racing is definitely a team sport.

Near the end of this race, Jeff and Dale Jarrett traded first place no fewer than four times, then actually exchanged paint going through the final turns. Jarrett slipped through for the win, but the second-place finish was enough to put Jeff back on top of the points standings.

Even so, Ray's warnings about Ford being given an edge had to be taken seriously. Ford cars had garnered eleven out of eighteen wins. Jeff had the other seven. Without the number 24 car, it would have been all Ford, all the time.

The next week Gordon was back at Indy. He drove an uncharacteristically slow qualifying time (twenty-fourth), so he was forced to play catch-up for the first half of the race. However, Jeff was patient, the Rainbow Warriors put on their usual competent performance, and he hung in there with a fourth-place finish.

On the Road Again

Gordon's second goal of the year was to win a road race. Road races don't award any more points than superspeedways or short tracks, of course, but for Jeff, it was a personal thing to show that he could be victorious on a road course.

On August 10 at the Bud at the Glen in Watkins Glen, New York, he got his chance.

The Bud is run on a 2.45-mile track, with no fewer than eleven S-turns, seven of which are right-hand ones (something Winston Cup drivers don't see very often, as they normally drive on ovals that always turn left). Driving this course is even more physically demanding than usual. Drivers have to brake, shift, and accelerate all day long.

Jeff's eleventh-place qualifying run was not the best precursor for a win, but it was the best he could do. There aren't a lot of places to pass at Watkins Glen, so it can be doubly tough coming from the back or even from the middle. However, Jeff patiently worked his way through, picking off drivers one by one. He didn't taste the lead until the race was more than half over, and he was immediately challenged by Dale Earnhardt, who covered the number 24 car like a shadow, then slipped past to retake the lead.

Jeff didn't lose his focus. He stayed on Earnhardt's rear and then, with twenty-seven laps remaining, reclaimed the lead for good.

A strong second-place showing at Michigan was followed by a migraine at the Goody's Headache Powder 500 in Bristol, Tennessee. Though Jeff qualified second and dominated the first half of the race, he and Jeremy Mayfield fought for the same patch of real estate on turn two, with disastrous consequences. Jeff passed a lapped Geoff Bodine and hit his gas at exactly the wrong time, crashing into Mayfield. The two cars crunched and Gordon rolled into the pits. He got back out on the track for a short while, then had to drop out completely, taking thirty-fifth and dropping behind Mark Martin in the 1997 points race.

Million Dollar Date

Following the debacle at Bristol, Team Hendrick received more sobering news. According to authors Shaun Assael in *Wide Open* and Robert Hagstrom in *The NASCAR Way,* as well as numerous newspaper reports, Rick Hendrick's health continued to deteriorate, so Hendrick decided to concentrate on his fight against leukemia, not against the federal government, and made a deal with prosecutors, offering a guilty plea for a single count of alleged mail fraud. The prosecutors recommended a $250,000 fine and ten to sixteen months home confinement.

Jeff always seemed able to pull out an emotional win when Hendrick needed one most. This was his chance to outdo himself. The upcoming Darlington race (August 31) was billed as the "Million-Dollar Date." Since Jeff had won the Coca-Cola 600 and the Daytona 500, a win here would net him the famous million-dollar bonus. Only one other driver, Bill Elliott, had (in 1985) ever collected such a prize. It certainly would be a great boost for the Hendrick team.

Jeff's car looked sharp, and the Rainbow Warriors donned customized T-shirts, building on the hype: "One driver. One team. One shot. One million."

The practice run gave the Rainbow Warriors hope—the car was running well, and though Jeff qualified only seventh on a track in which a driver really does not want to run in a pack, confidence remained high.

The green flag dropped and the bumping began. Dale Earnhardt mysteriously blacked out in his car in the first lap. It was a shock, to be sure, and doctors never were able to determine exactly what had happened.

It took Gordon seventy-two laps to gain the lead over the forty-two other drivers who had started the race. When he did so, the fans were electrified, on their feet, and excited about Gordon's chance to win a million dollars in a single day. The lead changed hands several times, and then, one hundred laps later, Jeff nearly lost it all. He raced by a spinning Ward Burton, just barely missing the number 22 MBNA car.

Soon Bill Elliott's McDonald's car was back out in front. Elliott would get the bonus points for leading more laps than anyone else, but Jeff's million-dollar bonus depended only on his leading the *last* lap. Elliott drove like he was determined to preserve his place as history's only million-dollar driver to date.

The weather cooled, making Jeff's car a little tighter, but the McDonald's car faded with the sun. Soon it was the two Jeffs—Gordon and Burton (Ward's brother)—battling it out for the lead. Gordon got a great final pit on lap 335, and was helped by a bungle in Burton's camp when somebody boggled a lug nut on Burton's vehicle. Jeff Burton came out of the pits in seventh place, but soon came roaring back. Both Ray and Jeff started getting nervous.

Gordon's car was becoming tight and extremely difficult to steer. Just then, Burton slipped behind him. The million dollars would be decided in the last lap and a half.

The two vehicles raced toward the white flag, and the final lap saw Gordon just barely holding on to his lead. As they took the white flag, the two Jeffs bumped, rubbed, and jammed each other without mercy. They were still touching as they crossed the start/finish line.

One lap to go.

It was clear that somebody would have to give. Gordon drove furiously to keep Jeff Burton behind him. "We were running for a million dollars and I wasn't going to let him get by me without a fight," Gordon recalled.

Burton's tires and car suffered most from the abuse of this contact racing, and he couldn't hold his position against Gordon's fierce determination, finally dropping behind on the backstretch. Gordon screamed in delight and rode number 24 around the track for a million-dollar payday. His winning margin was just 0.144 seconds.

Once again, the ailing Hendrick got the lift he badly needed from his star driver. And Jeff made it more than just emotional, promptly turning over $100,000 of his winnings to the Hendrick Marrow Program.

In addition to winning more than a million dollars, Gordon won an unprecedented third straight victory in the Southern 500, and he also regained the lead in the Winston Cup points standings for the 1997 season.

Autumn Angst

Jeff's lead increased to 97 points the next week, with a third-place finish in Richmond, Virginia. It was a Ping-Pong season as far as the standings were concerned, changing virtually every week, but one thing remained constant—the number 24 car was always right there in the top two or three. Now, with just eight races to go, Jeff only needed to figure out how to keep it that way.

It was still a bit early for the peak autumn colors in Loudon, New Hampshire, but the Rainbow car brought its own flash to fall in New England on September 14 for the CMT 300. It took Jeff half the laps—149 of 300 run—to take the lead for the first time, which he relinquished several times, but with just under seventy-five laps to go, Gordon took the lead for good.

It was the tenth victory of the season, and in the winner's circle, virtually everybody—including Brooke—held up both their hands with fingers spread.

Ten wins! The last driver to put together double-digit wins in a single season had been Bill Elliott, back in 1985.

Jeff qualified well—second place—the next week at Dover Downs, but after falling two laps behind, he was able to post just a seventh-place finish. Mark Martin won the race and inched up to Jeff in points. With six races left, Martin trailed Gordon by 105 points.

Gordon gave Martin another small window the next week by finishing fourth in the Hanes 500 at Martinsville, but Martin actually lost ground, finishing eleventh and falling back 30 points.

It was back to Charlotte on October 5 for the UAW-GM Quality 500. The three points leaders (Jeff, Mark Martin, and Dale Jarrett, in that order) all drove tough, tough races. Though Jeff once again qualified fourth, he never led a single lap, and Jarrett picked up ground on both of the top two leaders by winning the race. There were now just 125 points between first and second place—and Jarrett was still well within striking range, 197 points in back of Jeff.

With such a tight points standing, everyone was a little antsy about driving at Talladega (Alabama), the track where a wreck is all but guaranteed.

As it turned out, the points leaders had reason to be antsy.

All of them.

Jeff was the first casualty. He tasted the lead early on and was still in the lead pack when a blown tire stole control of his car and sent him careening into John Andretti. "I felt the left rear go just before my car turned sideways," he told the reporters who gathered around him. "Then I bounced off car 98 and just went spinning."

The number 24 car ricocheted into the wall, and the fans got a close-up view of the points leader's engine. Number 24 was virtually demolished—and both Martin and Jarrett had a golden opportunity.

Except that Talladega respects no one. *Boom, boom, boom! Crunch, smash, thump!* The pack crumpled against each other until literally half of the field was involved. It was an unmitigated disaster and, "fortunately" for Jeff, Martin and Jarrett were among the casualties.

After completely removing the hood and practically rebuilding Jeff's car, the Rainbow Warriors got number 24 back out into the action, hoping to salvage a few precious points. The car could move, but it couldn't race, and Jeff wasn't able to finish, though he did eke out a thirty-fifth-place finish—his worst showing since March 9. Martin picked up 15 points on Jeff; Jarrett 42.

The next week at Rockingham, Jarrett took second, Jeff was fourth, and Martin finished sixth.

The rest of the season would be character building for Jeff Gordon.

Guts

Another tire. Another blasted tire.

A stock car has thousands of parts. If any one part fails, trouble can result. You can work through a few malfunctions, but a tire will always take you down. A tire had taken Jeff out at Talladega, and a tire would do him in again.

The season's second-to-last race was motoring toward an end, with Jeff holding strong in fifth place. Then Gordon started telling Ray about a vibrating right front tire. Everybody in the pit immediately went on red alert.

With less than forty laps to go, the tire finally blew. Jeff immediately dropped twenty-five places, with Jarrett and Martin both running a strong race.

Evernham was apoplectic. "There were over two thousand tires here today and we got the only one that had a problem!" he lamented to reporters.

They got Jeff back out in thirtieth place, two laps down. The season was clearly on the line. Winning the race was out of the question, but Jeff was determined to hang on to his points lead.

Passing a car an average of every three laps, Gordon picked up thirteen positions and salvaged a seventeenth-place finish in what *Sports Illustrated* said, "might have been the gutsiest non-winning performance of his career."

Jeff's late charge was all the more important as Jarrett won the race and Martin finished sixth. The come-from-behind chase salvaged 39 crucial points for Gordon.

Championship on the Line

Jarrett was 87 points back, and Martin was 77 behind. If Jeff finished no worse than eighteenth at Atlanta—the final race of the season—there was no way either Jarrett or Martin could catch him. However, it's still unnerving to have two drivers with a chance to take the championship away from you in one race. Gordon would have to put on a good show in Atlanta. He couldn't count on both cars having a bad day.

The championship was by no means a lock. Jeff had finished worse than eighteenth seven times in the season, and he had placed seventeenth in the previous race.

Soon whispers started spreading about Gordon's tendency to fade. Remember what happened in 1995? some motorheads pointed out. Jeff had a 302-point lead with just four races left, and Earnhardt came within 34 points. A year later, in 1996, he led by 111 points going into the last four races and Terry Labonte won by 37 points. This year, he had led by 125 points with four races left.

Would history repeat itself?

With two blown tires in just three outings, Jeff shrugged his shoulders. "I don't know what to expect these days," he said.

Even Evernham was a little uncharacteristically antsy. "I was falling apart," he told Ed Hinton of *Sports Illustrated* (November 24, 1997).

Jarrett certainly wasn't conceding anything, saying he was "not cocky, just confident." Jarrett's crew chief, Todd Parrott, explained to reporters, "We're not the ones with the guns pointed at our heads. We're the ones pointing the guns."

Gordon viewed this as the most important race of his career, as it would determine whether he would be known as the type of driver who can win races but who can't clinch championships.

Weather reports presaged a dreary weekend as haulers pulled into Atlanta. As usual, Jeff's team brought two cars—the ideal car and a backup.

They'd need both.

Rains canceled Friday's qualifying, and Saturday bloomed cold and overcast. During Saturday practice, Jeff radioed the crew—prophetically, as it turned out—to let them know about the track. "Boy, it's so slick," he told Ray, "somebody is going to wreck out here."

Minutes later, coming into pit road at just 40 mph, Jeff started jerking the steering wheel back and forth to warm up the tires. His car suddenly spun 180 degrees, ramming Bobby Hamilton's parked Pontiac Grand Prix and demolishing the number 24's right front end. With the championship on the line and his best car ruined, Jeff called it a "bonehead" mistake on his part.

The Hendrick Motorsports team rushed into action, working feverishly to move the best engine into the backup car, *Backdraft*. In their rush, somebody overfilled the oil-cooler tank, which proved near disastrous for the qualifying run.

During the qualifying run, excess oil shot out of Jeff's exhaust pipes and onto the track. When the number 24 car's rear tires touched the oil, the car swerved. Jeff backed off the gas and managed to recover, but that slight hesitation was enough to give room for a full thirty-six drivers to crowd in front of him. It was Jeff's worse qualifying spot of the 1997 season.

All of a sudden, finishing eighteenth or better didn't sound so easy, especially since the crew figured that *Backdraft* was about a fifteenth-place car.

And Jarrett qualified third.

The Longest Night

The day should have been Jeff's coronation but now, according to his photo essay, it looked like it had been "scripted from a horror movie."

Even the track looked foreboding. The Atlanta Motor Speedway had been reconfigured and repaved, and the weather had allowed precious little practice time, meaning that all forty-three drivers would be reaching high speeds on a track that was virtually new to most teams. The expectation was obvious: numerous pileups early on.

That's not exactly good news when a driver qualifies in the back of the pack.

Jeff's anxiety was exacerbated by the fact that his "bonehead mistake" had taken out Bobby Hamilton's car as well as his own. Of all the teams to anger, why had he picked the one owned by legendary racer Richard Petty?

Gordon's accident plagued him all evening long, and he had a difficult time getting to sleep the night before the crucial event. When he finally climbed out of bed, he knew that within twelve hours he'd either be a two-time Winston Cup champion or NASCAR's newest choker.

Excruciating Finish

Backdraft never ran all that well. Though Gordon raced as high as tenth, he still needed to be calmed during the race. He just couldn't get the performance that he wanted from his car and kept radioing to Evernham what was wrong.

After a tire change, which caused Jeff to fall back to a precarious nineteenth place, the crew looked at his tires and sighed. They were worn down to the core. Since they hadn't managed to get fifty laps out of a single set of tires all day—and there were sixty laps left—Jeff would probably have to come in for an extra pit.

The championship was literally riding on a slice of rubber.

Ray had to make the call. If Jeff blew a tire now, he'd lose the championship. On the other hand, if he pitted while the other cars stayed out on the track, he'd probably lose it that way, too.

These are the moments when a crew chief earns his pay.

Ray decided to leave Jeff out in the action. If they were going to lose the championship, they were going to lose it on the track, not in the pits watching the rival cars go by.

In his photo essay, Jeff describes the harrowing conclusion: "Those last few miles were excruciating. . . . I spent the last ten laps trying to feel the tires under me. And I could feel them going away. They were all the way down to the cords. I was trying to keep them from blowing out. I was trying to keep them from spinning out. I was just racing my own race."

Things were getting really tight. Gordon couldn't slow too much because he was running in seventeenth place and Jarrett was driving like a man on a mission to steal the championship.

The entire season would be decided in a single lap.

"Even when they waved the white flag, I wasn't comfortable because I was afraid a tire could blow at any moment," Jeff told *Sports Illustrated*'s Ed Hinton. "Only when I came off turn four on the last lap and knew that I could get to the line even if a tire went, did I sigh in relief."

Jeff crossed the line in seventeenth place and Jarrett took third, giving Jeff the championship by all of 14 points.

Jeff's tires were absolutely shot.

Gordon, so often booed and jeered, got his share of adulation as he crossed the finish line. "I think they respect the Winston Cup champion," he told Hinton. Getting out of his car at the finish line Jeff jumped up on to the top of the car and took a celebratory leap into the air.

Bobby Labonte went to victory lane first for the race celebration, but the season belonged to twenty-six-year-old Jeff.

Celebration

The 1997 season points finish was one for the ages. Martin trailed Jarrett by just 15 points, so the three drivers had raced to the closest one-two-three finish and the fourth-closest one-two finish ever.

The fact that these three particular drivers had done so well showed the changing face of NASCAR. Instead of drinking away their anxieties—as many former NASCAR drivers would have done—Jeff explained, "Me and Dale and Mark got together last night, held hands, and prayed. And praying and having faith had a lot to do with what we were able to do today."

"We didn't get it done by a whole lot, but we got it done," Jeff added.

The season ending couldn't have come at a better time for Gordon, physically speaking. He checked into a hospital three days later to have a polyp removed from his vocal cords. The polyp was benign, and not uncommon among those who have to talk a lot for a living. And it gave Jeff a chance for a well-deserved rest.

"I don't know if I planned this surgery or if God planned it for me," he said, "but I'm going to have about seven to ten days here where I'm going to be able to do a lot of thinking. I'm really looking forward to that."

The Banquet

At the annual December banquet in New York, Jeff paid tribute to the owner who had believed in him early on. "Our whole goal for the season was to keep a smile on Rick's [Hendrick's] face and I'm sure that lifted his spirits, his third straight championship," Jeff said.

Jeff brought tears to many attendees when he started talking about how some people liked him, and some didn't. The stress of being so loved and so hated showed, and his emotions sprang up in front of everybody.

"When Jeff got up at the banquet," his mom told me, "if that didn't tell the whole world watching who he was, nothing ever will."

"He has to be who he is," Carol explained. "It's when you try to be something that you're not that you fail. That's why Jeff has always been so successful because he's never tried to be something that he isn't."

Jeff completed 11,988.62 of the 12,715.08 miles in the thirty-two Winston Cup races in 1997 and became the first NASCAR driver to exceed $4 million in regular-season winnings, taking home an astounding $4,201,227. To give you some idea of how the Winston Cup purses have grown, David Pearson, who is second only to Richard Petty with career wins (105), retired in 1986 with career earnings of $2.5 million. It took Pearson twenty-six years to earn just over half of what Jeff earned in one year.

Gordon received his second Driver of the Year award, joining Mario Andretti, Bill Elliott, Darrell Waltrip, Dale Earnhardt, Bobby Rahal, Bobby

Allison, and David Pearson as the only other multiwinners of racing's most prestigious honor. Jeff is the youngest individual ever to take two.

"Driver of the Year is very special to me," Gordon said. "And to even be thought of in the same sentence along with the previous winners, it just kind of blows me away when I think about it. It was a special year because of Rick Hendrick and to be able to put a smile on his face and help him forget what he was going through. We couldn't have asked for any more, and God certainly looked over us and blessed us."

The second title meant even more to Jeff than the first. "Nothing is sweeter than a championship, and I think the second time around is even sweeter," Gordon quipped, but his appetite to excel was far from quenched.

In fact, John Bickford uttered the words that should have put the other NASCAR drivers on notice: "Jeff's been winning races for a long time, and I haven't seen anything that tells me he's getting tired of it."

chapter 20

A Tough Start: February—May 1998

"I don't know that we'll win ten races again this season. Our plan is to eliminate mistakes, be more consistent, and win another championship."

—Jeff Gordon, 1998

Nineteen ninety-eight was NASCAR's fiftieth birthday. As the Winston Cup defending champion, Jeff realized the historic position in which he'd start his first race. "The sport has really moved up to another level and I'm proud to be part of it. I look forward to what it's going to be like at the one-hundredth anniversary. I hope I'm still around to celebrate," Jeff wrote in *Portrait of a Champion.* He would be seventy-seven years old, exactly the age of John Glenn as he returned to space. Maybe Jeff's hopes weren't so far-fetched.

But Jeff was realistic that 1997, with its ten wins, would be hard to beat. "Last year was definitely a career year," he offered. "When I'm older and look back on 1997, I'm going to wonder how it ever happened the way it did. . . . I don't know that we'll win ten races again this season. Our plan is to eliminate mistakes, be more consistent, and win another championship."

Dale's Daytona

Jeff had been responsible for ten of Chevrolet's eleven wins in 1997. If it hadn't been for the number 24 car, NASCAR would have been forced to give the

Chevy car some kind of a break. To keep any one make of car from becoming overly dominant, NASCAR frequently allows a model to be adjusted.

Now that the Hendrick team—driving Chevys—had won three championships in a row, the break fell to Ford. The new Taurus looked unusually good, taking the fastest time in the January test sessions on the Daytona track. In Ray Evernham's opinion, the specifications prescribed for the Ford cars gave them a decided advantage over every other model. If Ray and Jeff wanted to repeat, the story of their year would be finding a way to tame the Fords.

Miami Dolphins quarterback Dan Marino—one of NASCAR's newest team owners—waved the green flag to start Daytona in 1998. It was a signal of just how popular Winston Cup racing had become. Greg Sullivan, vice president of marketing for International Speedway Corporation (ISC), said, "You often hear [the Daytona 500] referred to as 'NASCAR's Super Bowl.' That's a nice compliment. But wouldn't it be great if, one day, the Super Bowl was referred to as 'the Daytona 500 of football'?"

If there was a hungrier driver in the field than Dale Earnhardt, you wouldn't know it. Despite Dale's legendary status, he hadn't won a race since March 1996. In that same period, Jeff had won nineteen times.

But it was Jeff who showed the early ambition. Though starting way back—twenty-ninth—he screamed into the front and was in the lead by lap 59. Number 24 was clearly the car to beat, and with a driver like Jeff behind the wheel, it looked all but certain that Jeff would take home his second Daytona victory.

But winning is never certain in the Winston Cup. About sixty laps after taking the lead, Jeff ran over some debris and sustained minor damage to the front of his car. Earnhardt looked like he had been raised from the dead. He jumped right back into the lead and drove with an angry attitude. Dale hung on to the lead, taking the white along with a yellow flag, and coasted to his first Daytona win. And guess what?

Dale "pulled a Gordon." The old man actually cried.

When the press had a field day with that one, Earnhardt corrected himself. "I don't think I really cried," he said. "My eyes watered up."

169

Jeff was gracious and generous in defeat, paying tribute to the man who deserved to finally win the big one. "We all would have loved to have been in victory lane," Gordon admitted, "but we're all really happy for Dale. If we couldn't be there, we all loved for him to be there. He's earned it, man. He deserves it."

Rockingham

Jeff's first win of 1998 came at the GM Goodwrench Service Plus 400 at the North Carolina Motorspeedway in Rockingham on February 22. He qualified in fourth place, which put him in the outside of row two, but experience was thin at the top. Ahead of him were Rick Mast, Kenny Wallace, and David Green, none of whom had won a series title. Rockingham favors a strong start—63 percent of the winners have begun the race in the first two rows.

The green flag dropped under ominous rainclouds. Though Jeff got a good start and was fourth after the first lap, he soon began dropping back due to tire problems.

Another pit thirty laps later gave the Rainbow Warriors a chance to install a spring rubber. The supposed fix—which didn't work—cost Gordon over twenty places. He came out of the pit with twenty-seven cars to pass if he wanted to take the lead—in a car that still wasn't operating right.

About twenty laps later, another caution gave the Rainbow Warriors a second chance to get Gordon's car in order. They took out the spring rubber and made other adjustments, and Gordon finally (after over a hundred laps) had a car that he could work with.

And he did.

Toward the end of the race, disaster nearly struck. The field erupted into a twisted-metal factory going into turn one. Top names—Jeremy Mayfield, Bobby Labonte, Ernie Irvan, and Dale Earnhardt, among others—crippled their cars, but Gordon and Wallace escaped unharmed.

That thinned the competition dramatically. Gordon without traffic is nearly uncatchable. He stretched his lead out over Wallace and raced into his thirtieth career Winston Cup victory and his second consecutive GM Goodwrench Service Plus 400 win.

Fighting the Fords

Jeff had a chance to make history the next week at the Inaugural Las Vegas by becoming the only driver in Winston Cup history to win three debut events. Only Lee Petty (who won inaugurals at Daytona and Richmond), Richard Petty (Dover and Pocono), and Buck Baker (Martinsville and Watkins Glen) had done what Jeff had done by winning at Indianapolis and Fontana. No driver in Winston Cup history has won three.

Unfortunately, an ill-handling car resulted in a seventeenth-place finish. Interestingly, just one Chevrolet finished in the top-ten. The new Fords looked pretty daunting, confirming the view of many (including Jeff and Ray) that they had an outright advantage.

A dreary postponed race in Atlanta on March 8, 1998, gave Jeff little practice time, and the results showed it—he finished nineteenth. After four races, Jeff was in seventh place in the points standing, trailing the leader (Rusty Wallace) by 147 points.

Darlington is usually a good track for Jeff, and though he qualified poorly (twenty-fourth), he managed to garner a second-place finish in the Trans-South Financial 400. That moved him up to fourth in the standings, but the Fords were so dominant that the usually upbeat Ray Evernham was already predicting defeat. He said that due to the Ford supremacy, any chance to repeat was "dead."

Say what?

Team number 24 moved into Bristol on March 29. It was a race full of cautions—fourteen in all. Rusty Wallace (driving a Ford) dominated most of the day, leading almost half the laps, but a cut tire and engine problems took him out of contention. Jeff never led until he came out of a pit on lap 437, but once in the lead, he never slipped back, holding off several late challenges to win the race and climb into third in the points standings, just 41 points behind Rusty.

Jeff gave the praise to the Rainbow Warriors. "The team deserves all the credit for this one," he said after the race. "We needed to bust off a good pit stop and we did it."

Two Fords finished first and second the next week at the Texas Motor Speedway in a race Jeff never really had a chance to compete in. A ten-car crash ensued and Jeff was among the casualties. The Rainbow Warriors got him back out on the track for a short spell, but all they could do was salvage a few points; Jeff finished thirty-first.

The poor showing dropped him to fifth in the standings, trailing the leader Rusty Wallace by 98 points. He dropped another 8 points the next week when he finished eighth at Martinsville. If Jeff was going to defend his championship, he'd have to find a way to beat the Fords.

Part of the problem was that Gordon wasn't getting any help on the track. Now that he was a two-time series champion, drivers were loath to cooperate with him—in a sport where drafting is an essential ingredient of success. If a teammate wasn't around, Jeff had a hard time finding a drafting partner.

During the closing laps the next week at Talladega, Jeff decided the time had come to make a move on the leader. He slipped out of the five-car train assuming—or at least hoping—that someone would be aggressive enough to go with him.

He was wrong.

Zoom, zoom, zoom, zoom—the cars slid past and Jeff looked like he had put the 24 car in reverse. Suddenly, the five-car train had just four cars, and Jeff's Rainbow was way behind. He was never able to recover in that race.

Jeff's earlier prediction that he might not garner ten wins in the 1998 season certainly was playing itself out. The season was one-fourth over, and Jeff had posted only one victory.

Things looked up on May 3 at the California Speedway in Fontana when Jeff won his first pole of the season. His fourth-place finish steadied his decline in the standings, but clearly, the first part of the season hadn't been what the Rainbow Warriors were hoping for.

Insult to Injury

On May 16 at the nonpoints Winston race in Charlotte, Jeff had a seemingly insurmountable ten-car-length lead going into the last lap. The race was his. But the motorheads started buzzing when the number 24 car flew into turn one and then started coasting into turn two.

What was Jeff doing?

Mark Martin thought Jeff was just playing with him, wanting to put on a show for the fans, but when he caught up Jeff didn't make a move. A stunned Martin passed Jeff, then realized the number 24 car was running out of gas.

Gordon had used up his gas on a NASCAR-mandated restart. They ruled that Jeff had accelerated too soon on the third leg, and the required restart was enough to deplete Jeff's fuel reserves—and cost him the race. It also cost him the first-place award of $257,500. Instead, Jeff had to settle for the "paltry" twelfth-place earnings of $83,500.

Would this season *ever* turn around?

Cookin' in Concord

The May 24 running of the Coca-Cola 600 was a race for the ages. Nobody dominated, the lead changed hands just about every time you blinked, and it took a total team effort to compete.

Jeff won the pole but lost the lead on the backstretch of the first lap. No worry; there were still 599 miles to go.

The first hundred laps provided fans with a stellar show as Jeff, Rusty Wallace, Mark Martin, and John Andretti traded the lead. It was a well-driven race, with good pits and solid competition—the kind motorheads dream of.

Pitting began almost immediately after lap 100, in reverse order, with the third-place car pitting first, the second-place car pitting second, and the first-place car pitting last (respectively John Andretti, Jeff Gordon, Mark Martin). Gordon's crew thought the car was running a little tight, so they made a chassis adjustment to loosen it up. Set free, Gordon pounced on Martin, retaking the lead off turn four on lap 124.

Jeff took two pits—one on lap 170 and one on lap 186, under a yellow flag—and it cost him. He was back in sixth place as the race neared its halfway mark. Worse, Gordon was pinned in heavy traffic and trailing several good drivers.

Driving the car like a surgeon cradles a scalpel, Gordon deftly maneuvered himself into fifth, and then fourth place. Thirty-nine laps after the halfway mark, Geoff Bodine went into a dangerous spin on the front stretch, right in front of Jeff. These are the moments when a driver doesn't have time to think; he just reacts.

His tires tasted grass as he shot low and touched the infield to evade the spinning car. When he got back on the track, he was in third place, but under a yellow flag. Everybody pitted. Jeff's next position was up to the Rainbow Warriors.

They gained him one spot. Jeff took to the track in second, sandwiched between Rusty Wallace and Dale Jarrett. There ensued a grueling battle for first place.

Within ten laps, Martin blasted by both Jarrett and Gordon to retake the lead on lap 267.

Then, with just twenty-two laps remaining, another yellow came out, and the leaders came in for the final pit. Evernham made a gutsy call. All of the leaders were taking on two tires and fuel; that was the well-known strategy that had saved Gordon time in a previous 600 and allowed him to win then. Ever the contrarian, Ray Evernham opted to take on four tires while the rest followed his old playbook and took on two. While that kept Gordon in the pit for a few additional (and precious) seconds, four tires would give Jeff's car another chance to compete against the faster Ford cars.

It was a gamble, sure enough, and Gordon found himself in sixth place by the time the green dropped with just fifteen laps to go. Jeff took fifth almost immediately, then tucked himself right behind Martin and Jarrett, blowing by them two laps later to take third.

Jeff and four good tires are a good bet to win anything, so Bobby Labonte and Wallace were no doubt sweating as Jeff closed in. Gordon continued to drive aggressively and took the checkered flag, five car-lengths in front of Wallace.

After the race, Gordon characteristically gave credit to the Rainbow Warriors and Evernham's gutsy call.

The Ford cars clearly showed their dominance that day by finishing second, fourth, and fifth. Evernham reflected, "There are things our team can do better to be competitive, but the Ford just is a better race car."

Jeff added, "I don't see too many other Chevrolets out there helping us out. The only real shot we had was taking on four tires against their two tires."

At any rate, Jeff's win put him in front of the points race for the first time in the 1998 season—three months behind his first lead in 1997.

Memories

The Winston came back to haunt Jeff the next week in Dover, Delaware. Though Jeff started second and led an obscene portion of the race—376 laps of 400—his quick pit (under a green flag) for a splash of gas with just seven laps to go bumped him back to a third-place finish.

The result was an unexpected win for Dale Jarrett, who had inhaled his share of Gordon's exhaust.

"We had to come in," Jeff explained to Kim Crawford of *Circle Track* (October 1998). "I think we were expecting those other guys to have to come in, too. We stretched it as far as we could possibly stretch it. We did everything we could do to try and win the race, but we can't jeopardize a top-five finish by trying to go for it. We'd much rather get those Winston Cup points."

After the race results were calculated, Jeff's points total of 1,765 gave him a slim lead of 47 over Jeremy Mayfield, but there was still a lot of season to go.

chapter 21

Mugged in Brooklyn

"Anybody [throwing padding] should be forced to run at Talladega Short Track for the rest of their life."

—Team owner Robert Yates, 1998

Just as the weather was getting hot, number 24 became a scorcher. It started on June 6, 1998, at the Pontiac Excitement 400 in Richmond, Virginia. Jeff qualified first with an astonishing track record, practically flying through the second lap.

Another factor working in Jeff's favor was the fact that Richmond would be a night race. "I like racing at night," Jeff told the media. "I've been racing at night ever since I can remember, even back in quarter-midget days."

But even a record pole and a favorable track don't provide any guarantees in the breakneck world of NASCAR, as Jeff would soon relearn.

The lead changed hands throughout the first two-hundred laps, with Jeff regularly fighting for the first spot. Uncharacteristically, Gordon began to get picked off by several drivers until he was sitting in fifth place.

There were just one hundred laps to go when Jeff radioed Evernham, expressing concern about his right rear tire. Evernham took no chances, calling for a full-service pit stop with four new tires, fuel, and a small track-bar adjustment. Despite all the tasks that had to be accomplished, the Rainbow Warriors still got Jeff out in an impressive eighteen seconds.

Their quick work sent Jeff back out in third place behind Rusty Wallace and Dale Jarrett, with just eighty-eight laps to go for the checkered flag.

Jeff fought his way to within one car-length of Wallace. Then, on lap 372, Gordon tucked in right behind Wallace. After figuring his car couldn't take Wallace low, Gordon shot for the outside. Jeff gained position, but Wallace refused to budge. His right front collided with Jeff's left rear, sending number 24 nose-first into the wall. The DuPont car sustained race-fatal damage to the right front and the radiator.

Jeff was furious. "It's pretty obvious," he told reporters. "Somebody can't stand to get passed, I guess. I came off turn two and I had the spot on him and he pinched me into the wall. We rubbed down the back straightaway. Then I finally get in front of him, and he just drives into the side of me and spins me out."

After Jeff climbed out of his smoking car and began walking toward the pits, some infield enthusiasts, who believed their $75 to $150 ticket gave them the right to say anything, went up to Jeff and said they were glad he had wrecked. Some even clapped maliciously, hoping to draw Jeff's attention.

"You try to ignore it," Jeff told Skip Wood of *USA Today* (October 31, 1998) about the ugly incident, "but at the same time you want to turn around and go after the person. But what you do is just let it roll off your back and say, 'Hey, I'm a bigger person that that,' and I know there are a lot of people . . . [who] appreciate the things I do."

The Rainbow Warriors' excellent work and Jeff's fine driving for all but eighteen of the 500 laps netted him no more than a disappointing DNF and a thirty-seventh-place finish, which dropped him from the lead in the points race.

Curious Caution

You can live with getting beat because of a flat tire, a blown engine, or an unavoidable wreck.

But roll-bar padding?

Throughout the first hundred laps, Jeff looked unbeatable at the Michigan Speedway in Brooklyn, Michigan, on June 14. The only time another car could gain the lead was when Jeff stopped for a pit; then he'd come back, reclaim the lead, and leave the others behind.

After Jeff built a commanding nine-second lead, it looked like he would run away with the race—and he probably would have, except that a controversial caution on lap 118 obliterated Jeff's gap and cost him the race. Jeff was furious about the caution, all the more so because, as he told Ray on the radio, he thought he had seen something "thrown" out of Jimmy Spencer's number 23 Taurus.

If a driver needs to catch up, there's no better friend than a caution, but NASCAR won't call a caution unless there's a wreck—or visible debris lying on the track. If a driver wanted a caution bad enough, he might be tempted to throw something on to the track to create debris, though this would be considered dangerous and completely unethical.

After the race, NASCAR surveyed the course and did indeed find three different pieces of roll-bar padding on the track. They immediately reviewed tapes of the race, but couldn't see if padding had been "deliberately" thrown, calling the tapes "inconclusive," though admitting the appearance of roll-bar padding was at least "suspicious."

To their credit, NASCAR took Jeff's charges seriously. Ray Evernham looked twice his size when he stomped over to the NASCAR trailer to complain about the caution. Winston Cup director Gary Nelson immediately got on the radio to his inspectors and told them to check out the cars driven by Jimmy Spencer, Bobby Labonte, and Darrell Waltrip and look for missing roll-bar padding. "If any of them have padding missing," Nelson said, "have them meet me in the NASCAR trailer after the race—driver and crew." But none of these cars were missing padding.

Robert Yates, a team owner for Jarrett and Kenny Irwin Jr. was strong in his denunciation. "Anybody doing that should be forced to run at Talladega Short Track for the rest of their life," he quipped, then suggested the guilty party should be "banned for life."

The padding controversy continued through the next week as the teams rolled into Pocono, Pennsylvania. NASCAR held a press conference and showed reporters the three pieces of roll-bar padding that had been found on the track. Two samples of padding had been split down the middle and fitted with Velcro—no problem to remove that, of course, as a simple yank would suffice. Another sample had been wrapped with duct tape, but get this—somebody had custom-fitted a thumbhole, which would allow the driver to pull it off easily if he wanted to create a false caution.

By showing the press what they found, NASCAR at least put the teams on notice—they were aware of what some teams were contemplating, if not doing.

The other news being discussed was Gordon's chance to become the first driver ever to win the Pocono race three years in a row.

Though Jeff won the pole, he fell one position short of winning the race, taking second to Jeremy Mayfield, who tallied his first Winston Cup victory. After his loss, Gordon told reporters, "[Mayfield] deserved it. We had nothing for him at the end. Jeremy did a great job. He's got the team; he's got the talent; he's got the attitude."

Top-Five Fever

Jeff was already well on his way to an amazing string of seventeen consecutive top-five finishes on the Winston Cup circuit. The year had gotten off to a rocky start, but Jeff was making up for lost time.

On June 28, the streak was threatened early in the race at the Sears Point Raceway in Sonoma, California, not far from where Gordon had first learned to drive as a little kid. Though Jeff began the race on the pole, rookie Jerry Nadeau had a brilliant start and immediately pulled ahead of Gordon, but the rookie's inexperience showed when he packed too much speed into turn two, a tight right-handed curve. His car swerved off course and almost took Jeff out.

Gordon pounced and retook the lead, with Jarrett tucked right behind.

"That first corner was pretty exciting, that's for sure," Jeff said later. "Jerry is an aggressive guy. He was just a little too aggressive, so we were happy to make it through that."

After Jerry Nadeau dropped back, Jeff's biggest nemesis was Bobby Hamilton in the Kodak car. On lap 96, Jeff got a fantastic run off turn ten and seemed poised to pass Hamilton for the lead.

The two drivers came up on turn eleven (a hairpin), and Gordon jammed his car inside on the tight turn. His car bumped Hamilton and Hamilton responded by bumping Jeff right back. Jeff won the pinball match as Hamilton went wide and Gordon pushed his car forward into the lead.

Hamilton fought back with fury, bumping Jeff in turn two on the next lap in a futile attempt to literally break his way back inside. He then pulled up next to Gordon at the hairpin where Jeff had passed him one lap earlier, glued to Gordon's rear bumper.

NASCAR immediately passed a message to the crew chiefs: "Tell the number 24 and the number 4 car to calm down."

Evernham opted not to pass along the message. "Hey, they're just racing," he told the official.

Jeff hung on to his lead and put himself back on top of the points standings.

After the race, Ray was asked about Hamilton and Gordon's tussle. "I knew my driver wasn't going to hit [Hamilton] back," Ray said. "When my driver is racing for the lead and the win, I am not going to pass [a warning] on." Then he looked back and saw a NASCAR official looking on with displeasure.

"I got busy," Ray added with a slight smile. "Yeah, so much was going on I got busy and just forgot to say something to Jeff."

Jeff's victory at Sonoma marked win 33 in his 172 career starts. He had now placed first at sixteen of Winston's twenty tracks; only Las Vegas, Texas, Michigan, and Phoenix remained unconquered.

chapter 22

The Streak

"Well, he came here to race, and now he's won two times. I think it's a true American dream. Back then, Jeff had nothing."
—John Bickford Sr., 1998

Just moments after Mark Martin climbed out of his Ford after the Pennsylvania 500 on June 21, 1998, he turned his hands to the sky, as if pleading for heavenly understanding. "I don't know where that 24 bunch has found that horsepower, but man, do they have the straightaway speed," he said. "Holy cow, does that thing go."

Martin had just watched Gordon and the Rainbow Warriors display their near total dominance. Jeff led a Pocono raceway record 164 of 200 laps and finished over a second ahead of Mark Martin, the second-place finisher.

"They gave me a great car today," Gordon said of his team.

Double Bricks

Even though the Brickyard is a relatively new race, it has gained an unusual prestige. John Andretti explained why to journalist Skip Wood: "You've got NASCAR, which is the major power in racing. You've got Indianapolis Motor Speedway, which is the greatest-known racetrack in the world. You put those two together, it's a formidable combination."

In fact, Andretti said he would now rank the Brickyard as one of the five great races, along with the Daytona 500, the Indy 500, the Monaco Grand Prix, and the twenty-four hours of Le Mans.

The Brickyard certainly draws fans. In fact, before the race Joe Gibbs, owner of Bobby Labonte's car and the former head coach of the Washington Redskins, pointed out that the crowd watching this race was two and a half times the size of any crowd he had ever coached in front of during a Super Bowl.

Indy is hallowed ground for Jeff. "Personally, just growing up around Indianapolis and going to the Indy 500, the Brickyard means just as much to me as the Daytona 500," he said.

Of course, there was also the matter of the money: "And the huge purse!" Jeff added.

The top-five finishers of the Coca-Cola 600—Jeff, Rusty Wallace, Bobby Labonte, Mark Martin, and Dale Jarrett—were all competing for the $1 million bonus, which would go to anyone who placed in the top five of a major event and then won the next one.

Before the race, all eyes seemed trained on Jeff. "I'd have to say that Jeff Gordon is the guy to beat," Ernie Irvan, the pole-sitter in his Skittles Pontiac car, told reporters.

The event consists of 160 laps around the two-and-a-half-mile rectangle, for a total of 400 miles. Jeff started third, behind Irvan and Jarrett, and immediately took second place, tucking behind Irvan.

For the first fourteen laps, most of the movement was in the back. Then Geoff Bodine touched a wall and scattered tire debris, bringing out the first caution, which sent every car in for a quick pit. Jeff was concerned that his car was pushing and asked Ray if they shouldn't go with four tires.

Ray opted for position instead. "Jeff, if you get up front, the push will go away," he insisted, and ordered a two-tire change, which sent the number 24 car out in first place on lap 18.

Gordon maintained the lead on the restart five laps later, then survived a challenge from Jeremy Mayfield. Mayfield's car looked formidable, but Jeff's quick driving kept him in front. But how long could he hold Mayfield off?

As it turned out, it didn't need to be for too long. On lap 35, Mayfield cut his right tire coming off turn one and bumped the wall, then spun and went head first back into the wall.

Once again, all the cars pitted, and this time, Jeff took on four tires. Even so, the Rainbow Warriors got him out in an almost unbelievably fast 16.5-second pit. Several other cars opted to take just two tires, so Jeff came out in fifth place; Ernie Irvan was back in the lead.

And then Jeff started passing, first one car, then another, and then yet another, to take second place. They weren't a match for Jeff with four fresh tires. Jeff couldn't fully focus on Irvan, though, as Jarrett was making a furious grab for second.

This got Ray concerned, so he jumped on the radio and cautioned, "Don't abuse the car, Jeff. *Save the car.* If you have to, let Jarrett go."

One lap later, Jarrett came up once again, and while Jeff didn't roll over, he did let Jarrett pass. Jarrett clearly had the car to beat.

With eighty-seven laps to go, Jeff dashed in for a green pit. Jarrett didn't follow, and while Jeff was sitting in his spot, Jarrett radioed his crew that he thought he was running out of gas. It couldn't have come at a worst time for Jarrett. He started rolling between turns one and two.

Gordon jumped back on the track while Jarrett struggled to move on fumes. Within seconds, Jeff had lapped his fiercest competitor, not once, but twice. Jarrett's car stalled about a hundred yards shy of his pit stop. Then followed one of the season's more comical moments as a group of heavyweight, potbellied crew members, chosen largely for their bulk and strength rather than their speed, ran out to literally push their driver into his pit stop.

Though Jarrett's crew frantically pushed him into the pits, the cars on the track were traveling 170–180 mph. Jarrett ended up losing four laps and went back out in thirty-seventh position. As Dale pulled away, his rear-tire changer collapsed and lay on the concrete, his head near a puddle of spilled gas. Other crew members had to help him back onto the wall.

To add insult to injury, Ward Burton's stopped car brought out another caution just after Jarrett made it back on to the track.

As the race wound down, fans got excited. A million dollars was on the line. During a caution at lap 118, Gordon took four tires in another phenomenal stop (16.6 seconds). Mark Martin's pit took a full five seconds longer than Jeff's. A lug nut popped off on the right front wheel, so Martin was cemented to his spot while Jeff raced forward.

Earnhardt, who opted to take just two tires, was in the lead on the restart. Jeff was in fourth, but not for long. He soon passed Bobby Labonte for third, then, half a lap later, passed Mike Skinner to take second. It took a little longer for him to catch Earnhardt, but with four tires to Earnhardt's two, it was inevitable that he would.

With about twenty-five laps to go, Gordon reported that he thought he saw oil on the racetrack. He was sporting a two-second lead over Labonte, and Ray didn't like what he heard. A caution was the last thing they wanted.

Some zealous crew members started to rush over to NASCAR to report the oil, but Ray stopped them. He shouted into the radio, "Hey, Jeff, we don't need a caution at this point; that's the worst thing that could happen."

Jeff dutifully responded, "What oil? I don't see any oil."

With twelve laps to go, it was looking good. Martin had the faster car, but Jeff was so far out in front it seemed that Martin would run out of time—until, two laps later, two cars broke down, bringing out a yellow flag and obliterating Jeff's lead. Now it was time for calculation. Martin was driving a faster car, and on the restart he'd be right on Jeff's bumper. Jeff radioed his motor man: "I need to know how hard I can turn this engine."

His car had two amplifier boxes; Jeff could flip to an alternative box, allowing him to go over 9,000 rpm. However, the engine had almost four hundred miles on it. Could it take the stress?

Without hesitation, the motor man shot back, "Switch over if you need to; it'll hold up."

The cars got ready for the restart. Three laps were driven under caution, meaning there would be just seven laps under green. One million dollars was on the line. Gordon, Martin, and Labonte were all eligible to claim the bonus, and they were running one-two-three.

Somebody was about to take home a whole lot of money.

When the green dropped, Jeff jumped away from Martin, quickly establishing about a half-second lead. And then, after just one revolution, Jimmy Spencer went into the wall on turn one, bringing out another caution.

When Jeff crossed the line under the yellow, he had completed 155 of 160 laps. There would be another restart.

The clean-up crews worked fast, and the pace car drove slowly so that the drivers would have a full three laps to race for the prized purse. The green dropped once again, and then all hell broke loose in the middle of the pack.

Five vehicles did not even make it to the start/finish line. They mixed it up right away, littering the track with vehicles (it looked like a disaster movie) and bringing out an immediate caution. With so many cars on the track and so few laps left, the race back to the yellow was really a race for the checkered flag and one million dollars.

It was a dangerous dash, but with a million dollars on the line and the Brickyard title up for grabs, the last thing Jeff was thinking about was safety.

The hometown crowd jumped to its feet and screamed as Jeff was the first across the line to complete lap 158.

The crowd's thunderous roar was overwhelming, leading Gordon to do something unusual. "When the race was over [and] I came down pit road, I actually shut off the engine. I had to hear it. I don't hear a roar like that anywhere else."

Sports Illustrated's Ed Hinton has pointed out that the "booing of Gordon's successes and the cheering of his failures (even his crashes) have reached the point of cruelty." So let the guy enjoy the unusual acclamation. He deserved it.

Three days before his twenty-seventh birthday, Jeff had become the first repeat winner of the Brickyard 400. Not only did he lead more laps than anyone else, he also clocked the fastest lap, a 172.180-mph scorcher.

The hometown boy not only pocketed over $600,000 for the win, but also the $1 million dollar No Bull Bonus.

Brooke got to share in the fun, joining Jeff in the back of a white convertible for several victory laps around the track.

After watching his stepson win, Bickford thought back to that moment in 1984 when Jeff was just eleven years old, one of hundreds of young fans hoping to get a signature from Rick Mears. That day, Jeff had promised his father that he would race here.

Surely the eleven-year-old couldn't have imagined earning a $1 million *bonus* in one day. The preteen also couldn't have anticipated becoming such a dominant force in NASCAR at such a young age.

The $1.64 million payout boosted Jeff past Bill Elliott and into second place on the all-time money-earned list of NASCAR Winston Cup racing. Gordon's $20.3 million to date was still well behind Dale Earnhardt's runaway $32.4 million, but being nineteen years younger than Earnhardt, Gordon has ample time to catch up.

Finding a Way to Win

Jeff has often said how much of a team sport racing is. On some occasions, his crew have helped give him a win that probably shouldn't have been his. On other occasions, Gordon has had to find a way to win in spite of his crew.

August 9, 1998, at Watkins Glen, New York, was one of those latter occasions.

The race couldn't have started out any better. Jeff won the pole and pretty much showed the back of the pack they would have to do something special to catch up to him. His car was running well and dictating the first two-thirds of the race, and Gordon seemed well on his way to winning his third consecutive victory.

And then came the pit on lap 59. Jeff came in and waited for the car to be dropped off the jack so he could take off.

In the pit for an interminable amount of time, Jeff watched in exasperation as his lead was stolen by Mark Martin and then buried as car after car exited the pits while the Rainbow Warriors kept working.

"I really don't know what happened in the pits", Jeff told the media afterwards, admitting—in a bit of an understatement, surely—I was a little disappointed at the time."

He came out in fifteenth place (ouch!) with two of the best drivers in NASCAR—Mark Martin and Rusty Wallace—in front of him.

Well, make that three. Ray Evernham decided not to tell Jeff that once he caught Mark and Rusty, he'd still have to chase after Mike Skinner. (Since Watkins Glen is a road course, it's a little more difficult for drivers to keep track of who is ahead of them.) "I figured he had his hands full," Evernham explained after the race. "After he got by them, there was seven laps to go, and I figured he still had time to catch Skinner."

Jeff chased, bobbed, and drove his heart out on the unusual, eleven-turn course that makes up Watkins Glen. He was focused on one goal, getting by Rusty and Mark. Rusty had slipped past Martin, whom Gordon also passed with just ten laps to go. When Jeff made his final pass by Wallace, there were just eight laps to go, and that's when he received the bad news.

He still wasn't in first place. He had to catch and pass Skinner in less than eight laps. It took him five, and he was helped in part by Skinner's gamble. With just a few laps to go, Mike was running low on fuel but decided to see if he could hang on. He had an imposing seven-second lead, usually more than enough on a road course like Watkins Glen, but his car's declining fuel proved to be his undoing. He had to slow down to conserve his gas, and Gordon was right there waiting for his moment.

Jeff's performance, coming back from a fifteenth-place position on a demanding course, put his colleagues in awe.

"Jeff was a smart driver today," Martin admitted to Mike Harris of the *Associated Press* after the race. "He gave us a driving lesson. He is just awesome."

Going for Four

Gordon came to Brooklyn, Michigan, on August 16 with three straight victories, though having never won on the Michigan Speedway. About 150,000 fans settled around the two-mile oval to see if Gordon could keep his streak alive.

187

Mark Martin was understandably the emotional favorite. Martin desperately wanted to win to honor his father, stepmother, and half-sister, who had recently died in a plane crash. Early on, it seemed like he would do it. The number 6 Valvoline car dominated the early part of the race, but with just twenty-one laps to go, Ward Burton blew an engine, brought the field together, and suddenly the race was up for grabs.

Gordon came into the pits in sixth and was astonished when he heard Evernham call out for just two tires. "I was shaking my head," Gordon said to Angelique Chengelis of *USA Today* (August 17, 1998) after the race. "I couldn't drive this thing with four good tires, and I didn't know what I was going to do with two."

But Evernham had faith in his driver, and just three laps after the restart, Gordon had wrested second place from Jarrett. Martin knew his nemesis was on his tail with just over ten laps to go. Gordon pulled up on the Valvoline.

"I just couldn't block him," Martin said. "I did what I could. I couldn't win . . . and I wanted to real bad. I had a lot of motivation, but I didn't have the stuff to do it today."

Gordon slipped by Martin on turn four of lap 191 and pushed his car to his fourth consecutive, and perhaps most improbable, first-place finish, becoming one of only seven drivers in modern NASCAR history to win four straight.

To Go Where No Driver Has Gone Before

On August 22, 1998, at the Goody's 500 in Bristol, Jeff had the opportunity to do what no man has yet to do in the modern era of the Winston Cup—take home a fifth consecutive victory.

Jeff qualified number seven; Rusty Wallace took the pole. When asked whether he was concerned about Jeff gunning for number five, he insisted he was not. "I've won three in a row before. It feels good when you're riding that wave, but at some point, that old horse will buck you off."

Gordon tried to downplay his run at history. "We're just trying to stay alive at Bristol," he told reporters. "If we're in contention in the closing laps, then we'll start thinking about winning five in a row."

Evernham has consistently credited Jeff's laser-sharp focus. Jeff is always thinking about the current turn, the current lap, the current challenge, content to let future records fall into place.

Ahead of Gordon in the fourth spot was the eager Mark Martin. Imagine how frustrating it must have been to rack up three second-place finishes and one fourth-place finish in a row as Gordon racked up four firsts. Gordon's DuPont rear bumper must have kept Martin awake late at night.

On the day of the race, Gordon was a bit ill, but he was feeling much better than his car, which he fought the entire race. It was an unruly vehicle, refusing to be tamed, handling poorly the full five hundred miles. For the first time in months, Jeff never led a lap, coming home in fifth.

"We had nothing for those guys," Gordon said afterwards to *USA Today* journalist Steve Ballard, which was reported in the newspaper's August 24, 1998, issue. "To come home fifth is a blessing. The five in a row was cool to go for. I would like to have won, but to come home in the top five, that's all we could ask for."

Martin's victory pared Gordon's lead from 97 points to 67, but he knew there was a real battle up ahead. "We know what we're up against," Martin admitted. "Trying to race against Jeff Gordon and Ray Evernham, it may turn out just like Michigan. This is just a baby step. . . . Jeff Gordon is, undoubtedly, one of the greatest race-car drivers to ever sit down in a car. I can't compete with his record."

That's an astonishing statement from a man good enough to be in the thick of a Winston Cup championship race. "In a lot of ways, I'm a Jeff Gordon fan," Martin admitted to Ballard after the race.

Even in his victory, Martin had to share the glory with Gordon. The next day, on the ESPN Sunday-morning radio program, an announcer proclaimed the winner of the Goody's 500 as "Mark Gordon." So intertwined was Jeff Gordon with victory that the faux pas was understandable. When Gordon's been the only name you've been talking about for weeks, it's hard to change habits.

But one owner in particular was fed up with Jeff's winning ways on the NASCAR tracks; he was about to launch the rubber row.

chapter 23

The Rubber Row

"Jeff Gordon has achieved things in the 1998 Winston Cup season that will be part of NASCAR lore, part of the tales people will tell when they talk about great drivers and astonishing deeds. And to think, the season isn't nearly over yet."

—Journalist Steve Waid, 1998

Most NASCAR races are supposed to pit forty-three drivers against each other, but in the summer and early fall of 1998, it seemed as if there were only two drivers who mattered: twenty-seven-year-old Jeff Gordon and thirty-nine-year-old Mark Martin. Virtually every week they battled it out for first and second, while everybody else argued over who would take third.

The New Hampshire 300 on August 30 in Loudon looked to be no different, though there were the occasional surprises. Twice Gordon got stuck on the outside of the track. When you do that at Loudon and no one lets you in, you might as well park your vehicle and call a cab. And as the points leader, Jeff didn't particularly qualify as a charity case. Fortunately, the first time it happened, teammate Terry Labonte came around and opened up a spot; Jeff slid in and made his way back to the front.

The second time it happened Terry wasn't there to let him back in. He went from second to seventeenth place in less time than it takes to sneeze.

But Ray Evernham and company had provided Gordon with a fast car. Once Jeff got back into the flow he started picking off positions.

Meanwhile, Martin looked determined, ultimately leading 193 laps out of 300. But sometimes, all it takes is one mistake. The last thing you want to do when you're running up near the front (and the number 24 car is struggling to catch up) is to bring out a caution, but that's just what Martin did, with about sixty-seven laps remaining in the race. Martin's car slid out, and Rich Bickle went into the wall trying to avoid hitting him.

Now it was Evernham time. Remember, there were still well over sixty laps to go. Evernham was confident enough in the car they were running that if Jeff could just get out of the pit in first place, he knew they could hold on for the win.

He sent Gordon back out with just two new tires. "Jeff hung with us," Ray said after the race. But sixty laps is a lot of track when everybody is coming at you with four fresh wheels.

"I just had to be easy on the tires," Jeff explained, while also admitting that with just two tires, he had his doubts about having the equipment to stay ahead of Martin.

As Ray planned, Jeff came out of the pits in first place, but everybody soon knew Jeff was riding on seriously diminished rubber. Martin bore down on Jeff with a vengeance. If he could get close enough to steal Jeff's air, he could create all kinds of trouble.

Finally Martin was in striking distance, within two car-lengths. With about thirty-six laps in the race, Evernham's gamble looked like it might not pay off.

But Martin went wide! He came out of a turn running too high and touched the wall. Jeff was off like a jackrabbit, and Martin was never a threat again. "I was trying to drive my car as fast as his and couldn't do it," Martin told reporters. "We had an incredible run, but we got outrun again."

And Jeff took home his fifth win in six races.

Roush's Rubber Row

Ford team owner Jack Roush watched Jeff pull away in New Hampshire and got a sour taste in his mouth. He was getting tried of watching his driver, Mark Martin, race to yet another second-place finish. Jeff had become so dominant that Roush apparently could come to just one conclusion: Jeff's team must be cheating.

The "whispers" around the track were that the Rainbow Warriors had discovered a chemical compound that made the stock tires softer, giving them a better grip on the track and allowing the vehicle to go faster.

According to Bill Weber of *ESPN Sportszone,* Roush charged archly, "The [number 24] car is running around there as a fourth- through tenth-place car on four tires and puts two tires on at the end and picks up seven- or eight-tenths [of a second]. That's really incredible. I don't know anyone else that can do that."

The racing world backed Jeff.

Dale Earnhardt, who knows what it's like to win consistently, immediately came to the Rainbow Warriors' defense. "They used to accuse us of cheating and having a company car," he told the media. "We heard it all. Gordon's bunch is hearing it now, but they've just got a good race team. Aerodynamics, engine program. Rick Hendrick has put a great group of guys together."

Roush was soon engulfed in a public-relations nightmare. Journalist Skip Wood reported in the September 9, 1998, issue of *USA Today* that Roush told a former NASCAR official and public-relations specialist, "You know all those things you taught me years ago? I managed to blow it all in one day."

Jeff's sister Kim works at a law firm in Charlotte, and everybody there was talking about the accusation. Carol Bickford (Jeff's mom), told me that a lawyer finally got up the nerve to ask Kim for her opinion. Kim looked the attorney in the eye and said, "Listen, my brother has been accused of cheating all his life. This is nothing new to him and it's not going to bother him a bit, I guarantee you.

"My brother and dad got protested when we were in quarter-midgets. We had our motors torn down, and I can remember staying late at half of the local races because someone was protesting my brother. This is nothing new to him, and they never found anything then and they'll never find anything now."

Kim went out to eat with Jeff, Brooke, and the Bickfords just a few days later, and when Kim recounted the conversation, Jeff laughed. "Yeah, I remember those days," he said.

Reflecting back on that time, Carol adds, "They would never give Jeff the credit."

Gordon may have taken it in stride, but Evernham was furious—a TNT television camera caught the normally mild-mannered crew chief storming over to Roush, getting in his face.

Referring to the tires, Evernham shot back, "It's just air, Jack, just air."

On the record, Evernham would eventually say, "I think [Roush's repeated claims are] a statement about how big his ego is. If somebody said that the only reason you can beat them is to cheat, what would you think? It sounds to me like Jack is losing his mind."

On the radio show *NASCAR Live*, Jeff said, "The only disappointing thing to me is Jack Roush kind of took away from our win," Jeff told the radio listeners. "I lost a lot of respect for Jack. I hope he'll apologize to our team. They don't deserve that."

NASCAR publicly disavowed the accusation. Spokesman Tim Sullivan said, "We don't believe that there's anything wrong with those tires, and we want to prove it." They confiscated Jeff's and Martin's tires, and sent them to a lab for testing.

Certainly, no one could accuse NASCAR of going easy on the Rainbow Warriors. Their post-race inspection, in the words of one eyewitness, "literally tore Gordon's car apart." *NASCAR Winston Cup Scene* (September 10, 1998), the premier NASCAR news publication, reported that NASCAR officials cut the tires and even took fuel out of the carburetor. They also cordoned off the pit areas so that the Rainbow Warriors wouldn't be allowed to tear down their own pit stall. Kevin Triplett, director of operations, said NASCAR sent Gordon's car "home in a bucket."

Jeff did not appear defensive. In fact, he even backed the impounding of the tires, saying, "We want everyone out there, not just in the garage but fans and everyone who watches the races, to know . . . we go out there and do it within the rules. If anyone is going out there cheating and getting away with things, I don't know how they could live with themselves afterward. Ray and the guys on our team have a conscience and we want to do it fair and square."

Roush was soon fighting this battle on his own. Mark Martin and his crew chief Jimmy Fennig both told Gordon, "Don't believe that's coming from us."

Evernham was grateful for Fennig's and Martin's support. "Through all this, I think the thing that's meant the most [is] Mark Martin and Jimmy Fennig are both good friends of mine and good friends of Jeff's. That friendship remains intact."

With public sentiment turned against him, Roush seemed humbled, and even publicly said he doubted NASCAR would find anything wrong with the tires. But to another reporter—Jeff Owens (*NASCAR Winston Cup Scene*)—Roush spoke the same story, disavowing the tire controversy, but implicating something else. "I would like to think the number 24 is not soaking their tires, but there is something really incredible going on with regard to the way they are able to do these miraculous late-race recoveries."

According to Owens, Jeff countered, "I hate it when people try to take away from a win. If they want to swap cars and go race, let's do it. People don't give enough credit to our team."

In fact, Gordon and Martin would swap cars, on the Tuesday after the New Hampshire race. It was during a tire test at the Atlanta Motor Speedway. Gordon explained to reporters that the idea was Goodyear's: "It's something that came up and Goodyear was kind of interested in doing something like that. [Martin] wanted to get in my car, and I wanted to get in his, so it was good for me to do and I think it was probably good for him to do, too."

A stock car is a very personal thing, set up to incorporate a driver's every preference. Jeff had a tougher time getting used to Martin's setup. "Mark's car was really loose and I wasn't as comfortable in his seat as I wanted to be, so I took it pretty easy in his car." But Martin "got right after it" (Jeff's words) in the number 24 car.

Evernham insisted that the car swap had nothing to do with the current controversy. "Jimmy and Jeff and Mark and I are all friends," Ray explained. "We just kinda wanted to see what each other had. We were a bunch of racers down there having a good time, working for Goodyear."

Dueling in Darlington

Another million-dollar bonus was on the line at the Pepsi Southern 500 in Darlington, North Carolina, on September 6, 1998. From the start, Roush's driver, Jeff Burton, looked like the man to beat. He put on a repeat performance of teammate Mark Martin's dominance the week before, leading for 273 of the race's 367 laps—including an opening tear, which had him in front for 242 of the first 274 laps.

The only time someone could get his car in front of Burton was when he was in the pits—and then he'd invariably take the lead back, as if he owned it and was only willing to let others play with it for a while. He mounted a seven-second lead during one stretch, and on another stretch, maintained his lead for a phenomenal 124 straight laps.

Jeff's car was running loose and the track was perilously slippery. "This was the hardest race I've ever had to run," Gordon recounted. "The car slid all over the place because the track was so slick."

During one pit, Jeff was exhausted by the heat. He was dizzy and his lips felt burnt. Steve Waid, writing for *NASCAR Winston Cup Scene* (September 10, 1998), caught the action.

"How many laps are left?" Gordon asked Ray during a pit.

"A hundred and fifty," Ray said.

Jeff wondered if he could make it.

The Rainbow Warriors tried everything, but Jeff couldn't catch Burton. "Jeff Burton just killed us all day long," Jeff told reporters after the race. But seeing Burton pull away struck a chord of inspiration in Gordon's mind.

"I realized what he was doing," Jeff said. "He was running his race and I had to run mine."

Jeff suspected that Burton's quick pull-away after the caution may have "used up his stuff." In fact, Burton's car did look a little looser. Jeff and Ray's strategy was to be patient, conserve their tires, and challenge late.

The strategy proved sound. When the race was about three-fourths over, the Rainbow car started edging up, even challenging Burton for the lead

And then, on lap 274, Gordon actually slipped by, going low. Jeff led for three dozen laps, then lost the lead during the pits.

But the stop did wonders for his flagging body. He dumped an entire water bottle over himself, then used a water-soaked rag to wash down his face and neck. It was enough to revive his energy. "I felt great when we went under that last green," he remembered.

Burton drove like there was no way he was going to give the lead back.

But, with just twenty-six laps to go, Gordon made his move on turn one, slipping down low and inside to take the lead for good.

Later Burton expressed his frustration. "I felt like I had won the thing," he told reporters. "We had a great race car, but just not when it counted. It got real loose toward the end."

Ward Burton, Jeff Burton's brother, was equally surprised: "I don't know how in the hell [the 24 car] beat my brother. Hell, in the last three or four races he's the only car on the racetrack. It's unbelievable. It's completely unbelievable. I wish I knew what they did to get that car to run like that. It was a hell of a run."

Jeff was putting his own unique stamp on 1998. He had won the same superspeedway race four years in a row. Even the King, Richard Petty, had never been able to accomplish such a feat in over two decades of racing—and Jeff had done it in just six full seasons! Even more impressive, Jeff became the first driver ever in modern NASCAR history to post three consecutive seasons with ten or more wins.

The victory also made Jeff considerably wealthier. Not only did he pick up the first-place earnings, but also his second million-dollar bonus. Further sweetening the pot, Martin's fortieth-place finish dropped him almost 200 points behind Gordon. Even so, the number 6 driver wasn't about to suggest that the overall points race was over: "It's just a little war that we lost, but the battle is still there."

The owner of Martin's car seemed less confident. "I'm pretty humbled by what happened," Roush confessed. "There's not much fight in me right now."

Gordon's spin was that Roush should think twice about getting Evernham angry. "Ray was pretty fired up," Jeff told reporters. "Things like what was said about us get us very fired up and motivated. I would suggest not to say those things. When this team gets fired up, watch out."

Cleared

"We've run every field test you can possibly run and their tires were fine," Winston Cup Director Gary Nelson announced the next week at a press conference. "There were ways to find what we were looking for, and we couldn't find anything that told us there was anything there."

Ray Evernham was vindicated and called for an end to the speculation. "I hope we can leave it here. . . ." he said to journalist Steve Waid.

The tire controversy finally quieted down as the haulers pulled into Richmond, Virginia, for the Exide 400 on September 12. It was the kind of ending that NASCAR was made for; the final twenty-eight laps were run without a caution, letting the drivers mix it up and race for the full glory.

With just five laps to go, the competition looked like another Roush nightmare—Jeff was driving his legal tires right up to Jeff Burton's bumper. But Burton hung tough on the outside groove of the track, which had proven to be the fastest line throughout the day. Though instinct tempts drivers to go low, experience often keeps them high at Richmond.

The intense dueling carried all the way through to the final lap at Richmond International Raceway. It was an exhilarating moment as Gordon raced into the final turn and just managed to get the front edge of his car even with Burton's door. This race would be decided by the length of a spark plug.

The two cars rocketed across the line. After four hundred miles, Burton's time was just 0.051 of a second faster than Gordon's.

The media described a "standing ovation," but in truth, there wasn't a fan in the raceway who had to stand to clap; everybody was already on their feet, leaning over to see who would take the checkered flag.

The reporters' first questions to Burton asked him to compare this race with the way he handled Gordon a year earlier at Darlington when Jeff won the million-dollar bonus. In both instances, each driver could have won the race by wrecking his competitor. "If I had a dollar for every time somebody had asked me why I didn't wreck Jeff Gordon at Darlington last year, I would have one million dollars," Burton said. In fact, Burton had reporters laughing with what he insisted was a true story.

"I pulled into town [in February] for the Daytona 500 to go get my physical. I pulled up to the guard out there at the tunnel, and the guard came running out and stopped me. He wanted me to roll my window down and I did and he said, 'How come you didn't wreck that Gordon boy at Darlington?'"

But Burton was reluctant to put too much emphasis on Gordon "paying him back," saying, more generally, "My point is that things come back around. . . . You race people the way you want to be raced. If you don't mind being rubbed, and knocking people out of the race, then do it. But understand they're going to do it back."

Though Jeff had placed second, he finished ahead of his nearest rival for the championship, Mark Martin, picking up another 5 points. But anything less than an absolute win made people wonder if Jeff was "playing it safe," going for points instead of first place. Gordon made it clear that wasn't the case.

"When you're going for a win, you forget about the points, especially that late in the race," he told Skip Wood of USA Today. "I was going for [the win]. I did everything I could. Maybe I could have taken some cheap shots at him, but that's not what it's all about. I like racing a guy hard and clean and trying to make a pass that way. Jeff Burton raced me the same way."

"Truly Remarkable"

At Dover the next week (September 20, 1998), it was all Mark Martin, all the time. He set a record with his qualifying time, and then proceeded to lead all but twenty of the four hundred laps. But as the race wound down, Jeff had a chance to make a race of it. The Dover fans jumped to their feet as Jeff methodically cut away at Martin's seemingly insurmountable lead. Then Jeff ran into traffic and Martin ran away, easily taking the win.

Jeff's second-place finish preserved his tight hold on the points race. Martin's victory remarks in the winner's circle were somewhat subdued when he reflected on his chances for the title. "We can win [the remaining seven races], and at this rate we won't be able to catch [Gordon]," he admitted.

By all accounts, it was an astonishing year. Early in September, Steve Waid, writing for *NASCAR Winston Cup Scene* (September 10, 1998), exulted, "[Jeff Gordon's] season has gone from good to very good, from very good to excellent, and now, from excellent to truly remarkable.

"Jeff Gordon has achieved things in the 1998 Winston Cup season that will be part of NASCAR lore, part of the tales people will tell when they talk about great drivers and astonishing deeds. And to think, the season isn't nearly over yet."

If only Waid had known what still lay ahead!

chapter 24

Phenomenal Finish

"Awesome! Awesome! Hey, Jeff, it's October, buddy, it's October."
—Crew chief Ray Evernham, 1998

The NAPA 500 on September 27, 1998, in Martinsville, Virginia, was a heat-baked affair. Temperatures flirted with a hundred degrees but settled around 95, making it 150 degrees inside the drivers' cars. It was a bail-out day, with many racers opting for relief drivers before the afternoon was done.

Jeff's best chance for a win came after a caution broke out with about fifty laps remaining. The winless-in-1998 Ricky Rudd was in the lead and trying to preserve his streak of sixteen seasons with at least one win (he succeeded).

"I drove as hard as I could," Gordon confessed afterward to Hank Kurz Jr. of the *Associated Press*. "It wore me out."

It wasn't enough for a win, but Gordon picked up 5 points on Martin, launching him into October with a formidable 199-point lead with five races left. Jeff proved that he could be as consistent in placing as he is dominating in winning—it was the fourteenth race in a row that Jeff finished in the top five.

As long as Jeff kept finishing well, Martin didn't have a chance. The biggest threat was a wreck, resulting in a low-thirties or -forties placement— which is why the Rainbow Warriors held their breath at Charlotte on October

4, 1998, as Bobby Labonte started an eleven-car altercation that ultimately resulted in brother Terry careening into the back of Jeff's car in turn two.

It was a hair-raising moment. "I was sideways," Gordon remembered after the race, to Steve Ballard of *USA Today* (October 5, 1998), "getting hit all over the place about two or three times. I don't know how I didn't get caught up in those wrecks."

Bumped but still running, Jeff eked out a fifth-place finish. Martin took the race, which would have made a DNF especially costly, points-wise, for Gordon.

"Do you feel like you dodged a bullet?" a reporter asked Jeff after the race.

"I feel like I dodged a six-shooter," Gordon joked.

Jeff had just completed his fifteenth straight race with a top-five finish. Even so, the media began harping on the fact that although Jeff had already won two Winston Cup championships and a phenomenal number of races, he had yet to win a race in October or November. When asked why this was so, Gordon snapped, "I think if we had the answer to that, we would have won in October or November."

But when pressed, Jeff admitted that it might have something to do with playing it, not safe, but a little more conservatively as title hopes loomed.

Now the Rainbow Warriors seemed intent on turning up the heat rather than just maintaining it.

"It seems like the other guys have brought out new cars and everything they could at the end of the season," Jeff offered, adding, "That's kind of our plan this year."

Taking Command

Jeff may have dodged the six-shooter in Charlotte, but he was back in battle the next week at Talladega. There is something almost malicious, perhaps even perverse, about building a superspeedway where cars can flirt with 200-mph speeds, and then mandating that cars who run on that fast track must have restrictor plates so they can't get away from each other. Drivers know exactly what pack racing at hair-raising speeds will lead to.

Geoff Bodine didn't qualify for the spring race at Talladega, so he got a chance to watch it. And what was he thinking?

"I was standing there, saying, 'All right, when's the wreck going to happen?'"

Though Jeff enjoyed a 174-point lead over Martin, Talladega stood like a specter ready to haunt him. If Jeff crashed and Martin won while taking 10 bonus points, Martin could actually put Gordon behind him. It was certainly no time to count on anything as won. Especially not with Talladega and Daytona being run back-to-back.

For a while, it looked like the racers might get away without any major altercations. They sped through 135 laps with no big pileups. Early on, Jeff's car looked strong, and he led for forty-nine laps. With just over fifty laps left, however, Jeff was in trouble. He was on the verge of going a lap down, uncharacteristically hanging back in twenty-fourth place. He needed a caution, bad, and he got it.

Ernie Irvan's car slowed down, Sterling Marlin came up from behind, and the two cars touched. At that speed, a touch is all it takes.

Irvan spun and was nailed by number 90, Dick Trickle, and—more significantly for the points race—number 6, Mark Martin. Eleven cars were involved by the time the metal stopped twisting.

Martin got back into the race, but managed to salvage just a thirty-fourth-place finish.

As Jarrett led the field, Gordon made a desperate solo chase, but his car just didn't have it. So he teamed up with Terry Labonte, the two drafting together in hot pursuit.

"Jeff and I were lined up behind him there," Labonte recounted to Skip Wood after the race, "and we couldn't close in on him any. That's kind of unusual. He was awfully strong."

Jarrett went on to win, with Jeff placing second and Terry third.

Martin took the opportunity to take a swipe at speedway/restrictor racing, which inevitably results in bunched-up fields. "If we had more than four of these a year, I'd find something else to do."

For his part, Gordon was understandably upbeat. "It was an up-and-down day, but there at the end, it ended up on the up side."

Suddenly Jeff was a seemingly insurmountable 288 points ahead of Martin with just three races to go. Even so, Gordon wasn't about to relax. He told journalist Skip Wood, "Just as easy as [a wreck] happened to [Martin], it can happen to me next week. We've just got to keep it going."

Breaking Through

Jeff did more than "keep it going" on October 17, 1999, for a Saturday-night race in Daytona Beach, Florida, the first night race ever held at Daytona. Still in search of that elusive October victory, Jeff waited until the race was half over before pushing his way into the lead, which he soon lost to Dale Earnhardt on a pit stop. The Intimidator kept the lead for forty-one laps, but Jeff worked his way around Dale with just thirty-seven laps to go on the 2.5-mile track.

He held it for thirty-two laps. But with five laps to go, just when Jeff was on the verge of finally getting a win in October, NASCAR opted to red-flag the race due to rain.

After a thirty-seven minute wait and a go-for-it three laps, Jeff took off in the lead. Bobby Labonte unleashed some spectacular driving and looked poised for a pass on the final turn, but nobody went with him and Jeff hung on for the win.

"Awesome! Awesome!" Ray shouted over the radio as he watched Jeff's car cross the finish line. "Hey, Jeff, it's October, buddy, it's October."

Jeff laughed. "You better believe it!" he said. "Yes it is. Yes it is."

Not only had Jeff finally won in the jinxed month of October, he accomplished something no NASCAR driver had ever done in the modern era—a record thirty-one wins in three seasons. Already, he had won eleven races this season.

"The only way we can win is if Jeff Gordon gets hurt, so I don't want to talk about it any more," Martin said. "People say it's mathematically possible, but practical people know it ain't going to happen."

Martin was right. Jeff had gained 70 points on Mark Martin, who finished all the way back in sixteenth place, which gave Gordon an insurmountable 358 point lead with three races left. Three thirty-second or better finishes in three races—which Jeff could do practically driving backward—would clinch the championship.

Top-Five Phenom

Rain. And more rain. Jeff's potential championship-clinching celebration was soaked through by an incessant shower that cut fifty-five laps out of the Dura-Lube 500 in Phoenix. Ironically enough, Rusty Wallace was least affected by the downpour, driving a car that seemed to have rockets behind the wheels. "It dominated," he admitted after the race. "Every single restart, I drove away. I don't ever think I've had a car that was that dominant for that long."

Gordon finished seventh, which left him one shy of breaking Pearson's record of eighteen straight top-five finishes. To show you how remarkable Jeff's string was, consider this: In the past seventeen contests, Jeff had finished 3–2–1–3–1–1–1–1–5–1–1–2–2–2–5–2–1.

Martin salvaged a second-place finish to keep himself in the running, but the gap between Jeff Gordon and the championship was narrower than a spark-plug setting. All Jeff had to do was finish fortieth at Rockingham.

Or just *start* the last two races.

In other words, Jeff could win the title showing up in a quarter-midget.

Jeff was about the only driver who refused to concede that the points race was a fait accompli. "It's not over until it's over, and as we've seen many times in the past, anything can happen."

When talking with reporter Skip Wood (*USA Today*, October 30, 1998), Jeff called 1998 "a dream season," the perfect plot for a movie where disaster strikes early but hard work, skill, and determination win the day. And Jeff made it clear that he was hoping to go out in Hollywood style.

He did it at Rockingham, creating a day to remember.

A "Killer" Day

Earlier in the year, during the spring race at Rockingham, the Rainbow Warriors had spent the entire day trying to give Jeff a car that had a chance to win. But in this race, the AC Delco 400, they came in with a car *(Butthead)* that they felt was a winner. If Jeff placed fortieth out of forty-three drivers, he would clinch his third championship.

Gordon's starting position of ninth wasn't particularly good news, though. Rockingham is notorious for chewing up tires, and this day the track was even more slippery than normal. While many drivers were bemoaning this, Evernham saw it as a plus for the number 24 car, pointing out that with Jeff's diverse experience on dirt tracks, sliding was nothing new to him.

Jeff fell back to eleventh place early on. He told Ray that his car was running a little tight, but once he got a better feel for it, he started passing cars and worked his way up to seventh.

With 273 laps to go, Kevin Lepage dropped out (Chad Little was already in the garage due to an earlier accident) and Gordon's championship was tantalizingly close—the worst he could place now was forty-second. And just as Jeff raced up to fifth place, Robert Presley took his car behind the wall.

There were now three cars out of action—but two of them could return.

Jeff wrested fourth from Mark Martin while Dale Jarrett and Rusty Wallace battled for the lead. After Rusty Wallace used traffic to take the lead from Jarrett, most cars broke for the pits.

Ray had Jeff stay out for another lap so he could pick up 5 bonus points for leading a lap, which meant he now just had to beat two cars. With one car already out, and another in the garage (Little was back out on the track), it was looking pretty good.

After his pit, Jeff was running in fourth place, still on the lead lap, but a hefty ten seconds behind Dale Jarrett.

And then, with just 206 laps to go, as Jeff raced in fourth place, Rick Mast announced he was out for the day. The Rainbow Warriors unfurled a banner next to Brooke that read: *1998 Champion NASCAR Winston Cup Series.*

Nobody under the age of thirty had ever won three Winston Cup championships.

205

Ray told Jeff the good news over the radio, but Jeff's reaction was focused on the race, not the season. "Man, I wasn't even thinking about that," he said after the race. "I almost wished they hadn't said anything about that because I thought it might break my concentration."

At that point, nobody could fault Gordon for taking it easy—having fun, basking in the moment. However, such an attitude didn't get him to the championship, and it wouldn't mark him beyond it, either. Jeff didn't slow down; in fact, he raced even harder, taking the lead.

With four laps to go, Jeff's 0.16-second lead looked comfortable, but Jarrett was driving with attitude and guts. Dale had posted four second-place finishes in the last five Rockingham races, and he didn't want another one; he was eager for a win.

That forced Jeff to drive hard as well. "I was actually locking the front brakes up getting into the corner because I was going in so hard," he commented after the race. "Jarrett was really, really fast. He was gaining on me in certain places. I wanted to make sure I didn't give up anything."

When the white flag dropped, Jeff was still way in front, but approaching traffic. Here was Jarrett's chance to pass Jeff and take the lead. Jeff expertly negotiated the lapped cars and went on to win by a half-second, becoming the first driver since Darrell Waltrip (in 1982) to win twelve races in a season.

Jeff rolled into victory lane, shouting as if it had been his first win. This wasn't feigned. Clearly, it still thrills Jeff to win. He high-fived the Rainbow Warriors as he rolled by, then paused and motioned for someone. Brooke raced up and gave the three-time champ a winning kiss.

It was the first time since 1994 that a championship had been clinched before the final race. Jeff jumped up on top of *Butthead,* then clambered down to give Brooke another kiss.

"Man, that was awesome," Jeff said to the television reporter. "Ray Evernham and the Rainbow Warriors, they are awesome; they are what has made this year the year that it has been." And then, in what has now become standard policy, Jeff also voiced appreciation for help of a more transcendent kind.

"God has been with us all the way. I just gotta thank him because I just know he's in my heart and blessing this team so much. What an awesome year; what an awesome championship!"

Topping off the Tank

Going into the last race of the 1998 season, Ray Evernham was exhausted. "Probably more tired than I've ever been in my life," he told Skip Wood of *USA Today* (November 5, 1998).

But it was a good tired, a vindicating fatigue, the kind that comes from a season well run. Though Evernham is now almost universally accorded the title of NASCAR's best crew chief, it wasn't that long ago that people doubted whether he had what it takes.

Now, with forty-one wins and three championships in an amazing six-year run, Jeff and Ray no longer had to "prove" themselves against some standard. They had become the standard. They were now the undisputed team to beat.

Remember, earlier in the season when Ray had said there was no way they could repeat as champions as long as the Ford cars were given an advantage? Well, midway through the season NASCAR reduced the allowed weight and size of the rear spoiler on the new Taurus cars. "If [NASCAR] had left the original rules there, we'd have gotten our butts kicked," Ray insisted.

With the championship locked up, Jeff rolled into Atlanta for the final race of the season. He was one victory shy of Richard Petty's modern-era record of thirteen victories in a single season, and he deeply desired to do well here. "What would cap this season off would be to run good at Atlanta and close out the season that way," he said before the race. "That to me would be the icing on the cake for 1998."

The race got started late due to weather, and suffered through two lengthy rain delays, keeping die-hard fans at the raceway for a good twelve hours. Gordon didn't lead the race until he chased down Dale Jarrett just six laps from the finish. This was a truncated ending; NASCAR got word of another storm just forty miles away and brought the NAPA 500 to a merciful—and, with Jeff's win, historic—finish.

Thirteen wins. . . . Now there really was no doubting whether Gordon would one day be mentioned in the same breath as Richard Petty, the King. At the very least, Jeff has certainly become the crown-prince-in-waiting.

Celebrate!

The season end provided little time to rest. NASCAR organized two exhibition races in Japan, and as soon as Jeff got back from Asia it was time to get ready for the banquet—which by now had become a weeklong affair for the champion.

Before Jeff arrived in New York, he found out he had been named 1998 Driver of the Year for the third time; Darrell Waltrip and Mario Andretti are the only other triple winners so far. And Gordon won the coveted title as decisively as he had won the championship—he was the *unanimous* choice of a fifteen-member nationwide panel of motorsports journalists.

Jeff began a whirlwind week in New York, arriving on Saturday, November 28. He and Brooke stayed at the Waldorf-Astoria and used the weekend as "downtime," taking in the *Nutcracker* at the Lincoln Center for the Performing Arts on Sunday.

There were myriad photo sessions and interviews on Monday, and television appearances all week long (including stints on the *Today Show* and *Live with Regis and Kathy Lee*). All the sports channels—radio and television—wanted their hour with Gordon, but Jeff didn't seem to mind.

"This is a pretty big deal because I don't think they've paid much attention to NASCAR in the past," he said.

There were also some charity engagements: a March of Dimes luncheon, for instance—and plenty of time to meet other celebrities, including Joe Torre, Olympian Kerrie Strugg, and Donald Trump.

The hottest ticket in town on Friday was for the banquet. Almost 1,500 people showed up at the Waldorf to celebrate the fastest stock-car drivers on the planet. Jeff's close-to-$3-million bonus for winning the championship pushed his season earnings to over $9 million—and that doesn't count endorsement income.

In his speech—spoken without any tears this year—Jeff paid tribute to Rick Hendrick. (Rick was still ailing; his cancer was in remission, but due to his slow recovery he still would not be able to attend such events as the 1999 Daytona 500.) "My biggest regret was that Rick Hendrick couldn't be in victory lane with us this year," he said. He also thanked Ray Evernham, Brooke, and God, among others. He then joined some of his colleagues for a smaller party, with Kool and the Gang providing entertainment.

The year of Gordon's dominance was certainly storybook caliber. His consistency was unnerving, racking up twenty-six top-five finishes overall (a modern-era record). His ability to win has become legendary, as he tied Richard's Petty's twenty-three-year-old record of thirteen victories in a single season. And his ability to win consistently—no other driver in the modern era of NASCAR has ever posted the most victories four years straight—is unsurpassed.

Jeff Gordon, once called the Kid, has now become NASCAR's leading *man*.

chapter 25

Dynasty: 1999 and Beyond

"He's the prototype of the future driver, groomed for it since he was a little kid. He doesn't throw his helmet and cuss NASCAR when something goes wrong; he just goes back to work. The guy's a great driver."

—Darrell Waltrip, 1997

"Some people write history with ink. Others with burning rubber."

—DuPont ad celebrating Jeff Gordon's 1998 championship

At the start of Jeff Gordon's seventh full season of NASCAR racing, there appeared to be no stopping him. He became a two-time winner of the Daytona 500 on February 14, 1999, giving himself the points lead from the very first race of the season, with a thrilling and fearless 190 mph pass by Rusty Wallace in the final laps.

A few dips followed, including a hard solo crash in Texas on March 28 (caused by a poor-handling car that "just wouldn't turn") which severely bruised Jeff's ribs and chin; an unavoidable accident at Talladega in April (Jeff was T-boned by Rusty Wallace); and uncharacteristic engine trouble in several races.

But the bright spots showed Jeff and the Rainbow Warriors are still the team to beat. Gordon notched another win at the Cracker Barrel 500 in Atlanta in March, and posted his forty-fifth career win (and NASCAR-leading third win for the season) at the California 500 at the end of April.

Just before the spring race in Charlotte, rival drivers were still picking Jeff to win the title, even though he was fifth in the standings.

"Even based on what's happened so far," driver Kyle Petty told USA Today's Skip Wood in the May 28, 1999 issue, "it's tough to bet against that 24."

Rival car owner Felix Sabates told Wood essentially the same thing: "I really believe when it's all said and done, Jeff Gordon will win it again. Momentum is everything, and talent and skill and luck is the rest of it, and he's got it all. He's a great race-car driver and he's got a great team and he's got momentum and he doesn't choke."

Whatever hunger keeps Jeff Gordon and Ray Evernham going shows no sign of being satisfied.

In 1998, *Racing Milestones* asked driver Mark Martin, "What do you think is more important in Winston Cup racing: youth and exuberance or experience and cunning?" Martin replied, "I think both. And I think that you have that with Jeff Gordon. It's rare when you get both in one person. Youth and enthusiasm, along with skill, will get you a long way."

Charlotte Motor Speedway president Humpy Wheeler sees big things in store for Jeff. "He's got the potential of doing what athletes like Palmer and Ali, Joe Namath and Babe Ruth and DiMaggio did, and that is to transcend the sport they're in."

Jeff's mom Carol told me she is sure of one thing: "He's not through setting records. He's done that all of his life. In fact, he probably still has records that stand in quarter-midgets. Where can Jeff go? It's unlimited. I'm sure he'll break Richard Petty's record of seven championships. There's no doubt in my mind—assuming he doesn't decide to leave racing early."

She adds, though, "I don't think it's ever been a goal in Jeff's life to beat Richard Petty's record. I don't think that's what Jeff is all about. I think Jeff Gordon is more about being who he is and if [beating Petty's record] happens, then so be it."

Whatever the future, Jeff Gordon is enjoying the present. "I'm very fortunate, very blessed," he told Skip Wood of *USA Today*, "that my life has turned out the way it has. I'm very happy with my life, and if other people can't understand why I'm happy or resent the fact that I am, that's something I can't control."

"I don't know that I'll really comprehend what it all means until later in life," Jeff said, late in 1998, "when I can sit back and look at everything we've accomplished."

That's understandable. It's difficult to write history while you're making it.

Jeff Gordon and the Rainbow Warriors are entering the rarefied air of a dynasty, rivaling the 1990s' Chicago Bulls, the Yankees in the 1920s, or the Boston Celtics in the 1960s.

How long can this go on? "If I have years like I had this year [1998], I'll race as long as I possibly can," Jeff said.

Evernham, who knows Jeff as well as anybody, doubts that 1998's spectacular success has dulled Jeff's appetite. In fact—and this should strike genuine fear in the hearts of would-be competitors—Ray thinks it may even create more motivation.

"What motivates Jeff . . . is the next race," Ray explained to journalist Dick Brinster. "It seems the better you do, the more you get motivated."

If that's the case, watch out—nobody will have more motivation in the years ahead than Jeff Gordon.

Glossary

Backstretch: The back straightaway on an oval, located between turns two and three, on the opposite side of the start/finish line.

Banks: The pitch of a curve on a racing oval, which ranges from a mild 9-degree bank at Indianapolis to a steep 36-degree bank at Bristol. On a 36-degree bank, the car will slide down the track if it is not going at least 90 mph. Road courses do not have banked curves.

Black flag: A black flag is unique among flags in racing, in that it is waved at an individual car rather than the entire field. It signifies that the driver has broken a rule and must get off the track.

Busch Grand National Series: A series of races for stock cars just under the level of the Winston Cup. This is the "minor leagues," where less experienced or less skilled drivers or newer teams compete until they are ready for the Winston Cup series.

Caution: Whenever a wreck occurs or debris litters the track, officials will wave a yellow flag, signaling a caution, under which all the drivers must slow down to about 55 mph (they follow a pace car). Drivers are not allowed to pass other cars on the tracks during a caution, though they may gain an advantage if the cars pit and a driver gets back out on the track sooner than someone else.

Checkered flag: The flag waved when the winner crosses the finish line.

DNF: Stands for "Did Not Finish"; given to a driver who fails to complete the race.

Green flag: Signifies that the race can proceed at full speed. It is waved at the start of the race and whenever the race is resumed after a caution or interruption.

Lapped: A driver is "lapped" whenever he is already trailing the leader and is passed once again. If, for instance, a driver is in a lengthy pit stop and the field circles the track five times before he comes back out, he is lapped five times, or is "five laps down." To get back into the lead, he would have to pass the leader five times.

Loose: When a car's steering is called "loose," it means that the car has a tendency to slip or slide too far out when the driver turns the wheel. A "tight" car is the opposite—it tends to be unresponsive to a driver's attempt to turn.

Motorhead: Slang for a NASCAR fan.

Pace car: The car that leads the racers around the track during a caution and at the start of the race.

Pit or pit stop: An area on the inside of the track where cars come in to be adjusted and fueled. The most advantageous pit stop on most tracks is the last one.

Pole: The front starting position, given to the fastest qualifier. Cars line up in 22 rows, two abreast. The pole is the bottom car in the first row.

Qualifying: Two laps that are run a day or two before the race. The fastest lap determines a driver's starting position, with the fastest driver starting up front.

Red flag: A red flag signifies that a race is being stopped. All drivers are to get off the track.

Relief drivers: NASCAR rules allow a substitute driver to complete a race in a car started by whichever driver qualified. The driver who started the race is credited with the points earned, regardless of who finishes the race.

Restrictor plate: This is a metal plate, attached near the carburetor, that restricts the amount of airflow to the engine. This, in turn, reduces a vehicle's available horsepower. Restrictor plates are used only on superspeedways, ostensibly as a safety device, but many drivers feel they make racing more dangerous. Since restrictor plates strip a car of its ability to get a sudden burst of power, drivers are less able to shoot around wrecks or break away from a pack.

Splits: Interval times taken during a race or during the two qualifying laps.

Tachometer: A panel instrument that measures an engine's revolutions per minute.

Tight: See "Loose."

Victory circle/lane: The specially designated spot on the infield where winners are honored and awarded their trophy.

Voltmeter: A panel instrument that measures electrical force.

White flag: Signifies that the race leaders have just one lap to go.

Winston Cup Series: A 34-race series (in 1999) for the elite, premier level of NASCAR racing.

Yellow flag: Signifies a caution; all cars must slow down and follow the pace car.

Bibliography

Author Interviews

Carol Bickford (September 17, 1998)

John Bickford Sr. (September 17, 1998)

Books

Assael, Shaun. *Wide Open.* New York: Ballantine Books, 1998.

Brinster, Dick. *Jeff Gordon.* Philadelphia: Chelsea House Publishers, 1997.

Gordon, Jeff. with Bob Zeller. *Jeff Gordon: Portrait of a Champion.* New York: HarperCollins Publishers, 1998.

Hagstrom, Robert. *The NASCAR Way.* New York: John Wiley and Sons, Inc., 1998.

Hemphill, Paul. *Wheels: A Season on NASCAR's Winston Cup Circuit.* New York: Simon and Schuster, 1997.

Holder, Bill, and Jeff Gordon. *An American Racing Fantasy: The Story of Jeff Gordon.* Self-published book, no date or imprint given.

Huff, Richard. *Insider's Guide to Stock-car Racing.* Chicago: Bonus Books, 1997.

Mair, George. *Natural Born Winner: The Jeff Gordon Story.* New York: Ballantine Books, 1998.

Stewart, Mark. *Jeff Gordon.* New York: Grolier Publishing Company, 1996.

Articles

"Bonus-Baby Gordon Wins Southern 500 Again." *Seattle Times,* September 7, 1998.

"Brickyard Remains Jewel for Gordon." *Associated Press,* August 1, 1998.

"Gordon Can't Afford to Coast to Cup Title." *Washington Times,* October 11, 1998.

"Gordon Makes History." *Tacoma News Tribune,* November 2, 1998.

"Gordon, Martin Swap Cars for a Day." *NASCAR Winston Cup Scene,* September 10, 1998.

"Gordon Says His Team Deserves an Apology." *Associated Press,* September 2, 1998.

"Jeff Gordon." *People,* May 12, 1997.

"Jeff Gordon." *Ragged Edge Race Report,* June 6, 1998

"Martin Ends Gordon's Bid for Record." *Seattle Times,* August 23, 1998.

"Million Dollar Man." *CNN/SI,* posted September 7, 1998.

"Racing for a Reason." *Tacoma News Tribune,* September 20, 1998.

"Results Plus." *New York Times,* October 7, 1996.

"To Fuel or Not to Fuel." *Racing Milestones,* October 1998.

"Turn Four." *NASCAR Winston Cup Scene,* September 10, 1998.

"Wallace Takes Goody's 500 Pole." *Bellingham Herald,* August 22, 1998.

Adler, Jerry. "Chariots of Fire." *Newsweek,* July 28, 1997.

Ballard, Steve. "Man and Machine." *USA Today,* August 21, 1998.

———. "Martin Halts Gordon with Win, Kind Words," *USA Today,* August 24, 1998.

———. "Martin Swerves Wrecks for Charlotte Win." *USA Today,* October 5, 1998.

———. "Martin's Winston Cup Hopes Crash." *USA Today,* October 12, 1998.

———. "Wonder Man." *USA Today,* August 5, 1998.

Berggren, Dick. "Why Fans Boo Jeff Gordon." *Stock-car Racing,* October 1998.

Bornhop, A. "NASCAR '95." *Road and Track,* February 1996.

Bourcier, Bones. "Why Hendrick Wins." *Stock-car Racing,* January 1997.

Brinster, Dick. "Burnout Among Biggest Issues for Gordon." *Associated Press,* November 12, 1998.

———. "Martin Outpaces Gordon at Dover." *Associated Press,* September 21, 1998.

Chengelis, Angelique. "Gordon Rallies for Victory." *USA Today,* August 17, 1998.

Crawford, Kim. "The Coca-Cola 600." *Circle Track,* October 1998.

———. "The MBNA Platinum 400." *Circle Track,* October 1998.

———. "The Winston." *Circle Track,* October 1998.

De Jonge, Peter. "Fast Times in Stock-car County," *National Geographic,* June 1998.

Dunn, Jeff. "God's Speed." *New Man,* March–April 1996.

Dutton, Monte. "What's in a Car Name?" *Charlotte Motor Speedway Collector's Edition Magazine,* May 1998.

Gannett News Service. "Gordon Wraps Up Title." *Bellingham Herald,* November 2, 1998.

Glick, Shav. "The Coronation of the New." *Los Angeles Times,* November 3, 1998.

———. "Gordon Can Say Thanks a Million." *Los Angeles Times,* August 2, 1998.

Goldberg, Steve. "Smile, You're a Winner." *Time,* June 15, 1998.

Hamilton, Don. "High Jinks on High Banks." *Racing Milestones,* October 1998.

Handelman, David. "Speed Freak." *Details,* September, 1997.

Harris, Mike. "Despite Pit Fall, Gordon Devours Watkins Glen Field." *Associated Press,* August 10, 1998.

Hershey, Steve. "Gordon Closes in On Third Cup Title." *USA Today,* October 19, 1998.

Hinton, Ed. "The Hunt's Over." *Sports Illustrated,* February 23, 1998.

———. "It Wasn't Pretty, But . . ." *Sports Illustrated,* November 24, 1997.

———. "A Million to One." *Sports Illustrated,* August 10, 1998.

———. "On the Fast Track." *Sports Illustrated,* April 24, 1995.

———. "Riding Shotgun with Jeff Gordon." *Sports Illustrated,* August 18, 1997.

———. "Safety in Numbers." *Sports Illustrated,* February 24, 1997.

Hoover, Terry. "Love Makes the World Go Round . . . and Round . . . and Round . . ." *Carolina Bride,* January–March, 1995.

Kurz, Hank, Jr. "Rudd Fends Off Heat to Extend Record Season Win String." *Associated Press,* September 28, 1998.

McCraw, J. "The Making of a Winston Cup Champion." *Popular Mechanics,* April 1996.

Mooney, Loren. "Pit Strategy is the Difference." *Sports Illustrated,* June 1, 1998.

O'Leary, Mike. "Sir Wins a Lot." *Racing Milestones,* October 1998.

Owens, Jeff. "From Sickbed to Second-place." *NASCAR Winston Cup Scene,* September 10, 1998.

———. "'Tiregate' Controversy Heats Up." *NASCAR Winston Cup Scene,* September 10, 1998.

P-I News Services. "Gordon Survives Bump, Wins Race." *Seattle Post-Intelligencer,* July 27, 1998.

———. "Unstoppable Gordon Wins Again." *Seattle Post-Intelligencer,* August 17, 1998.

Poole, David. "Clean Racing Has Its Rewards for Burton." *Charlotte Observer,* September 14, 1998.

Rodman, David. "Gordon Caps a Phenomenal Championship Season." *NASCAR Online,* December 4, 1998.

———. "Gordon Continues to Raise the Bar." *NASCAR Online,* December 4, 1998.

Rodman, David, and Tim Sullivan. "Jeff Gordon's Champion's Diary." *NASCAR Online,* November 30, 1998.

Rusz, J. "Daytona 500." *Road and Track,* May 1997.

Scully, Mary. "What Happened to Good Sportsmanship?" *Racing Milestones,* October 1998.

Siano, Joseph. "At Daytona Rookie Looks like Favorite." *New York Times,*
    February 14, 1993.

———. "A First at Indy for an Indiana Home Boy." *New York Times,* August 7, 1994.

———. "From Wonder Boy to Leader." *New York Times,* July 16, 1995.

———. "Gordon Goes All Out and Finishes in Style." *New York Times,*
    December 10, 1995.

———. "Gordon Hears the Roar of the Hometown Fans." *New York Times,*
    August 8, 1994.

———. "NASCAR Releases Schedule." *New York Times,* September 5, 1996.

Tresniowski, A. "Appeal at the Wheel." *People,* June 30, 1997.

Voegelin, Rick. "The Natural." *Sport,* February 1995.

Waid, Steve. "Gordon Rules the Rock." *NASCAR Winston Cup Scene,* March 2, 1995.

———. "It's Another One for Gordon." *NASCAR Winston Cup Scene,* September 7, 1995.

———. " A Million More." *NASCAR Winston Cup Scene,*
    September 10, 1998.

Weber, Bill. "NASCAR Impounds Gordon's, Martin's Tires." *ESPN Sportszone,* no date.

Williams, Deb. "Gordon and the 'Rainbow Warriors.'" *Winston Cup Scene,*
    December 7, 1995.

———. "Gordon Snares Third Win of '95." *Winston Cup Scene,*
    April 6, 1995.

Wire Reports. "Gordon's Crew Gambles on Tires; He Delivers Victory." *USA Today,*
    August 31, 1998.

———. "Gordon Wins Pepsi 400." *USA Today,* October 18, 1998.

Wood, Skip. "Brickyard 400 Carries Weight." *USA Today,* July 30, 1998.

———. "Burton Edges Gordon at Exide 400 Wire in Clean, Heated Duel." *USA Today,*
    September 14, 1998.

———. "Daytona, Marlin a Good Match." *USA Today,* October 16, 1998.

———. "Focus Drives Gordon's Chief." *USA Today,* November 5, 1998.

———. "Gordon Claims Race, Third Season Crown." *USA Today,* November 2, 1998.

———. "Gordon in Place to Deliver Crowning Blow . . ." *USA Today,*
    October 30, 1998.

———. "Gordon Is Class of Pennsylvania 500 Field." *USA Today,*
    July 27, 1998.

———. "Gordon Strives for Five." *USA Today,* August 20, 1998.

———. "Gordon Takes Charge of Winston Cup Race." *USA Today,* September 8, 1998.

———. "Gordon's Victory Thrills Indy Crowd." *USA Today,* August 3, 1998.

———. "Jarrett Holds Off Gordon, Who Adds to Lead On Martin." *USA Today,* October 12, 1998.

———. "Mr. Perfect." *USA Today,* July 31, 1998.

———. "NASCAR Restrictor Plates Bring out Pack Mentality." *USA Today,* October 9, 1998.

———. "Rahal Picks Papis for His Car in '99." *USA Today,* September 1, 1998.

———. "Richmond Primed for More Drama." *USA Today,* September 11, 1998.

———. "Rivals Wary of Gordon's Winning Ways." *USA Today,* May 28, 1998

———. "Roush Begins to Rue Tire Talk." *USA Today,* September 10, 1998.

———. "Talladega Drafts Key to Racing Strategy Sunday." *USA Today,* October 8, 1998.

———. "Wallace Is Singing in the Rain." *USA Today,* October 26, 1998.

Index

INDEX

About the Author

Gary L. Thomas has written or cowritten nine books and over seventy-five articles. He has worked with numerous celebrities—including Heavyweight Boxing Champion Evander Holyfield—on their own books. His book with Senator John Ashcroft was a finalist for the Gold Medallion Award. Mr. Thomas is well published in the fields of athletics, politics, and religion. He makes his home in Washington State.

Also available from
RENAISSANCE BOOKS

The Sandman: An Autobiography
by Karch Kiraly with Byron Shewman
ISBN: 1-58063-054-5 • $22.95

The Complete Book of Sports Nicknames
By Louis Phillips & Burnham Holmes
ISBN: 1-58063-037-5 • $12.95

Three Dog Nightmare
by Chuck Negron as told to Chris Blatchford
ISBN: 1-58063-040-5 • $22.95

Tim Burton: An Unauthorized Biography of the Filmmaker
by Ken Hanke
ISBN: 1-58063-046-4 • $22.95

BOOKS

To order please call
1-800-452-5589